The Merchant of Venice

BY WILLIAM SHAKESPEARE

PRESTWICK HOUSE
LITERARY TOUCHSTONE CLASSICS™
P.O. Box 658 • Clayton, Delaware 19938

SENIOR EDITOR: Paul Moliken

EDITORS: James Scott, Anna Gonzales, Cassie Ash, Chelsea Phillips, and Bob Jones

COVER DESIGN: Wendy Smith

PRODUCTION: Jerry Clark

PRESTWICK HOUSE
LITERARY TOUCHSTONE CLASSICS

P.O. BOX 658
CLAYTON, DELAWARE 19938
TEL: 1.800.932.4593
FAX: 1.888.718.9333
WEB: www.prestwickhouse.com

13 WEST BEVERLY STREET
STAUNTON, VIRGINIA 24401
TEL: 1.540.885.5588
FAX: 1.540.885.4886

Prestwick House Teaching Units™, Activity Packs™, and Response Journals™ are the perfect complement for these editions. To purchase teaching resources for this book, visit www.prestwickhouse.com/materials

ISBN: 978-1-58049-163-1

CONTENTS

STRATEGIES FOR UNDERSTANDING SHAKESPEARE'S LANGUAGE 4

READING POINTERS FOR SHARPER INSIGHTS 9

DRAMATIS PERSONAE 10

Act I
    SCENE I 11
    SCENE II. 16
    SCENE III 19

ACT II
    SCENE I 25
    SCENE II. 26
    SCENE III 31
    SCENE IV 32
    SCENE V. 33
    SCENE VI 35
    SCENE VII 37
    SCENE VIII. 39
    SCENE IX 41

ACT III
    SCENE I 45
    SCENE II. 48
    SCENE III 56
    SCENE IV 57
    SCENE V. 60

ACT IV
    SCENE I 63
    SCENE II. 75

ACT V
    SCENE I 77

GLOSSARY 86

VOCABULARY 90

Strategies for Understanding Shakespeare's Language

1. **When reading verse, note the appropriate phrasing and intonation.**

    DO NOT PAUSE AT THE END OF A LINE unless there is a mark of punctuation. Shakespearean verse has a rhythm of its own, and once a reader gets used to it, the rhythm becomes very natural to speak in and read. Beginning readers often find it helpful to read a short pause at a comma and a long pause for a period, colon, semicolon, dash, or question mark.

Here's an example from *The Merchant of Venice*, Act IV, Scene i:

The quality of mercy is not strain'd, *(short pause)*
It droppeth as the gentle rain from heaven
Upon the place beneath: *(long pause)* it is twice blest; *(long pause)*
It blesseth him that gives, *(short pause)* and him that takes; *(long pause)*
'Tis mightiest in the mighties; *(long pause)* it becomes
The throned monarch better than his crown; *(long pause)*

2. **Reading from punctuation mark to punctuation mark for meaning.**

    In addition to helping you read aloud, punctuation marks define units of thought. Try to understand each unit as you read, keeping in mind that periods, colons, semicolons, and question marks signal the end of a thought.
    Here's an example from **The Taming of the Shrew**:

    > LUC. Tranio, I saw her coral lips to move,
    >   And with her breath she did perfume the air;
    >   Sacred, and sweet, was all I saw in her.
    > TRA. Nay, then, 't is time to stir him from his
    >   trance.
    >   I pray, awake, sir: if you love the maid,
    >   Bend thoughts and wits to achieve her. (I,i)

    The first unit of thought is from "Tranio" to "air":
    He saw her lips move, and her breath perfumed the air.

The second thought ("Sacred, and sweet...") re-emphasizes the first.

    Tranio replies that Lucentio needs to awaken from his trance and try to win "the maid." These two sentences can be considered one unit of thought.

3. In an **inverted sentence**, the verb comes before the subject. Some lines will be easier to understand if you put the subject first and reword the sentence. For example, look at the line below:
    "Never was seen so black a day as this:" (Romeo and Juliet, IV, v)

You can change its inverted pattern so it is more easily understood:

"A day as black as this was never seen:"

4. An **ellipsis** occurs when a word or phrase is left out. In *Romeo and Juliet,* Benvolio asks Romeo's father and mother if they know the problem that is bothering their son. Romeo's father answers:

*"I neither know it nor can learn of **him**" (Romeo and Juliet I,i).*

This sentence can easily be understood to mean,

"I neither know [the cause of] it,
nor can [I] learn [about it from] him."

5. As you read longer speeches, keep track of the subject, verb, and object – *who* did *what* to *whom.*

In the clauses below, note the subject, verbs, and objects.

Ross: The king hath happily received, Macbeth,
    The news of thy success: and when he reads
    Thy personal venture in the rebel's fight... *(Macbeth* I, iii)

1st clause: *The king hath happily received, Macbeth,/The news of thy success:*
SUBJECT – The king
VERB – has received
OBJECT – the news [of Macbeth's success]
2nd clause: *and when he reads/thy personal venture in the rebel's fight,*

SUBJECT – he [the king]
        VERB – reads
        OBJECT – [about] your venture

In addition to following the subject, verb, and object of a clause, you also need to track pronoun references. In the following soliloquy Romeo, who is madly in love with Juliet, secretly observes her as she steps out on her balcony. To help you keep track of the pronoun references, we've made margin notes. (Note that the feminine pronoun sometimes refers to Juliet, but sometimes does not.)
But, soft! what light through yonder window breaks?
It is the east, and Juliet is the sun!
Arise, fair sun, and kill the envious moon,

Who* is already sick and pale with grief,   *"Who" refers to the moon.*
That thou her* maid art more fair than she:*   *"thou her maid" refers to Juliet,*
                                                                                the sun.
                                                        "she" and "her" refer to the moon.

5

In tracking the line of action in a passage, it is useful to identify the main thoughts that are being expressed and paraphrase them. Note the following passage in which Hamlet expresses his feelings about the death of his father and the remarriage of his mother:

> O God! a beast that wants discourse of reason
> Would have mourn'd longer – married with my uncle,
> My father's brother, but no more like my father
> Than I to Hercules. (I,ii)

Paraphrasing the three main points, we find that Hamlet is saying:

- a mindless beast would have mourned the death of its mate longer than my mother did
- she married my uncle, my father's brother
- my uncle is not at all like my father

If you are having trouble understanding Shakespeare, the first rule is to read it out loud, just as an actor rehearsing would have to do. That will help you understand how one thought is connected to another.

6. Shakespeare frequently uses metaphor to illustrate an idea in a unique way. Pay careful attention to the two dissimilar objects or ideas being compared.
   In *Macbeth*, Duncan, the king says:
   > I have begun to plant thee, and will labour
   > To make thee full of growing. (I,v)

   The king compares Macbeth to a tree he can plant and watch grow.

7. An *allusion* is a reference to some event, person, place, or artistic work, not directly explained or discussed by the writer; it relies on the reader's familiarity with the item referred to. Allusion is a quick way of conveying information or presenting an image. In the following lines, Romeo alludes to Diana, goddess of the hunt and of chastity, and to Cupid's arrow (love).

   > ROMEO: Well, in that hit you miss: she'll not be hit
   > with Cupid's arrow, she hath Dian's wit;
   > and in strong proof of chastity well arm'd (I,i)

8. Contracted words are words in which a letter has been left out. Some that frequently appear:

be't	on't	wi'
do't	t'	'sblood
'gainst	ta'en	i'
'tis	e'en	
'bout	know'st	'twill
ne'er	o'	o'er

9. Archaic, obsolete and familiar words with unfamiliar definitions may also cause problems.

   - **Archaic Words** Some archaic words, like *thee, thou, thy*, and *thine,* are instantly understandable, while others, like *betwixt,* cause a momentary pause.
   - **Obsolete Words** If it were not for the notes in a Shakespeare text, obsolete words could be a problem; words like "beteem" are usually not found in student dictionaries. In these situations, however, a quick glance at the book's notes will solve the problem.
   - **Familiar Words with Unfamiliar Definitions** Another problem is those familiar words whose definitions have changed. Because readers think they know the word, they do not check the notes. For example, in this comment from *Much Ado About Nothing*, the word *an* means *if*:

       Beatrice: Scratching could not make it worse, *an* 'twere such
       a face as yours were. (I,i)

     For this kind of word, we have included margin notes.

10. Wordplay: puns, double entendres, and malapropisms

    - A *pun* is a literary device that achieves humor or emphasis by playing on ambiguities. Two distinct meanings are suggested either by the same word or by two similar-sounding words.
    - A *double entendre* is a kind of pun in which a word or phrase has a second, usually sexual, meaning.
    - A *malapropism* occurs when a character mistakenly uses a word that he or she has confused with another word. In *Romeo and Juliet*, the Nurse tells Romeo that she needs to have a "confidence" with him, when she should have said "conference." Mockingly, Benvolio then says she probably will "indite" (rather than "invite") Romeo to dinner.

11. **Shakespeare's Language**

    The following text is adapted by special permission from Ralph Alan Cohen's book, *Shakesfear and How to Cure It—A Guide to Teaching Shakespeare.*
    What's so hard about Shakespeare's language? Many students come to Shakespeare's language assuming that the language of his period is substantially different from ours. In fact 98% of the words in Shakespeare are current-usage English words. So why does it sometimes seem hard to read Shakespeare? There are three main reasons:

    - Originally, Shakespeare wrote the words for an actor to illustrate them as he spoke. In short, the play you have at hand was meant for the stage, not for the page.

- Shakespeare had the same love of reforming and rearranging words the same as hip-hop artists and sportscasters do today. His plays reflect an excitement about language and an inventiveness that becomes enjoyable once the reader gets into the spirit of it.

- Since Shakespeare puts all types of people on stage, those characters will include some who are pompous, some who are devious, some who are boring, and some who are crazy, and all of these will speak in ways that are sometimes trying. Modern playwrights creating similar characters have them speak in similarly challenging ways.

Stage Directions:

Prestwick House and the American Shakespeare Center share the belief that Shakespeare's stagecraft went hand-in-hand with his wordcraft. For that reason, we believe it is important for the reader to know which stage directions are modern and which derive from Shakespeare's earliest text—the single-play Quartos or the Folio, the first collected works (1623). All stage directions appear in italics, but the brackets enclose modern additions to the stage directions. Readers may assume that the unbracketed stage directions appear in the Quarto and/or Folio versions of the play.

Scene Locations:

Shakespeare imagined his play, first and foremost, on the stage of his outdoor or indoor theatre. The original printed versions of the plays do not give imaginary scene locations, except when they are occasionally mentioned in the dialogue. As an aid to the reader, this edition *does* include scene locations at the beginning of each scene, but puts all such locations in brackets to remind the reader that *this is not what Shakespeare envisioned and only possibly what he imagined.*

Reading Pointers for Sharper Insights

Take note of the following when reading *The Merchant of Venice:*

1. One of the significant aspects of this play, as in all of Shakespeare's plays, is the poetic beauty of the language in the extended metaphors, similes, puns, etc. Shakespeare's language, especially in his use of metaphors often expresses an insightful comment on the human condition, which makes them all the more valuable

    Take the time to figure out the meanings of these metaphors and similes. Frequently, they will help you understand the play, as well as life in general.

2. Although there were not many Jews in England in the sixteenth and seventeenth century, anti-semitism, which had always been present in medieval England, rose to a fever pitch when the Queen Elizabeth's physician, Dr. Rodrigo Lopez, a Portuguese Jew, was hanged for plotting with the Spanish to kill her.

    The depiction of Shylock, the stereotypical Jewish villain—characterized by an excessive love of money and the desire to injure a Christian through trickery—pandered to this anti-semitism. But note how Shakespeare develops Shylock. Of all the characters in the play, he is, by far, the most fully developed and has the greatest emotional range.

    Finally, note that Shylock is an outsider. For the Elizabethans, who believed that the social order was ordained by God, the outsider was a threat to the harmony of society. Shakespeare echoes that opinion, but does give Shylock some of the most moving lines in the play.

3. Although usury was legal in England at this time, it was frowned upon and looked down on by most of Elizabethan society. There were restrictions against money-lending in the Church, and Shylock would, therefore, have been despised, not only because he was a Jewish outsider, but also because he lent money and charged interest on it. Audiences would have held a societal prejudice against his character prior to seeing the play.

4. Note the development of these themes in *The Merchant of Venice*:
    A. Justice: Should justice be tempered with mercy, or should it be above emotion and implemented just as the laws decreed?
    B. Friendship: How important is it? What is its role in this play?
    C. Love: What characterizes true love?

DRAMATIS PERSONÆ

ANTONIO, a merchant of Venice

SALERIO,
SALANIO, } *friends, to Antonio and Bassanio**

BASSANIO, his friend, suitor to Portia

LORENZO, in love with Jessica

GRATIANO, friend to Antonio and Bassanio

PORTIA, a rich heiress

NERISSA, her waiting-maid

SHYLOCK, a rich Jew

THE PRINCE OF MOROCCO, suitor to Portia

LAUNCELOT GOBBO, a clown, servant to Shylock

GOBBO, father to Launcelot

LEONARDO, servant to Bassanio

JESSICA, daughter to Shylock

THE PRINCE OF ARRAGON, suitor to Portia

TUBAL, a Jew, his friend

BALTHASAR, servant to Portia

THE DUKE OF VENICE

STEPHANO, servant to Portia

Nobles of Venice, Officers of the Court of Justice, jailer, servants, and other Attendants, messenger.

*Note: Numerous spelling variations exist for Antonio's friends.

ACT I

[SCENE I]
[Venice]

Enter Antonio, Salerio, and Solanio.

ANTONIO: In sooth,[1] I know not why I am so sad;
 It wearies me; you say it wearies you;
 But how I caught it,[2] found it, or came by it,
 What stuff 'tis made of, whereof it is born,
5 I am to learn;
 And such a want-wit[3] sadness makes of me,
 That I have much ado to know myself.
SALERIO: Your mind is tossing on the ocean;
 There, where your argosies, with portly sail,—
10 Like signiors and rich burghers on the flood,
 Or, as it were, the pageants of the sea,—
 Do overpeer the petty traffickers,
 That curt'sy to them, do them reverence,
 As they fly by them with their woven wings.
15 SOLANIO: Believe me, sir, had I such venture forth,
 The better part of my affections would
 Be with my hopes abroad. I should be still
 Plucking the grass, to know where sits the wind;
 Peering in maps, for ports, and piers, and roads:
20 And every object that might make me fear
 Misfortune to my ventures, out of doubt
 Would make me sad.
SALERIO: My wind, cooling my broth,
 Would blow me to an ague, when I thought
25 What harm a wind too great might do at sea.
 I should not see the sandy hour-glass run,
 But I should think of shallows and of flats;
 And see my wealthy Andrew† dock'd in sand,

1truthfully

2the sadness

3foolish, witless

†Terms marked in the text with (†) can be looked up in the Glossary for additional information.

Vailing her high-top lower than her ribs,†
30   To kiss her burial. Should I go to church,
And see the holy edifice of stone,
And not bethink me straight of dangerous rocks,
Which, touching but my gentle vessel's side,
Would scatter all her spices on the stream,
35   Enrobe the roaring waters with my silks,
And, in a word, but even now worth this,
And now worth nothing? Shall I have the thought
To think on this; and shall I lack the thought
That such a thing, bechanc'd, would make me sad?
40   But tell not me; I know, Antonio
Is sad to think upon his merchandise.

ANTONIO: Believe me, no; I thank my fortune for it,
My ventures are not in one bottom trusted,
Nor to one place; nor is my whole estate
45   Upon the fortune of this present year:
Therefore my merchandise makes me not sad.

SALANIO: Why, then you are in love.

ANTONIO: Fie, fie!

SALANIO: Not in love neither? Then let us say, you are sad,
50   Because you are not merry: and 'twere as easy
For you to laugh, and leap, and say you are merry,
Because you are not sad. Now, by two-headed Janus,†
Nature hath fram'd strange fellows in her time:
Some that will evermore peep through their eyes,
55   And laugh, like parrots, at a bag-piper;
And other of such vinegar aspect,
That they'll not show their teeth in way of smile,
Though Nestor† swear the jest be laughable.

Enter Bassanio, Lorenzo, and Gratiano.
Here comes Bassanio, your most noble kinsman,
60   Gratiano, and Lorenzo: Fare you well;
We leave you now with better company.

SALERIO: I would have stay'd till I had made you merry,
If worthier friends had not prevented me.

ANTONIO: Your worth is very dear in my regard.
65   I take it, your own business calls on you,
And you embrace the occasion to depart.

SALERIO: Good morrow, my good lords.

BASSANIO: Good signiors both, when shall we laugh? say,
        when?

70   You grow exceeding strange: must it be so?

SALERIO: We'll make our leisures to attend on yours.

                           Exeunt Salerio, and Solanio.

LORENZO: My Lord Bassanio, since you have found Antonio,

      We two will leave you; but at dinner-time,

      I pray you have in mind where we must meet.

75 BASSANIO: I will not fail you.

GRATIANO: You look not well, Signior Antonio;

      You have too much respect upon the world:

      They lose it that do buy it with much care:

      Believe me, you are marvellously chang'd.

80 ANTONIO: I hold the world but as the world, Gratiano;

      A stage, where every man must play a part,

      And mine a sad one.

GRATIANO: Let me play the fool!

      With mirth and laughter let old wrinkles come;

85   And let my liver rather heat with wine,

      Than my heart cool with mortifying groans.

      Why should a man whose blood is warm within

      Sit like his grandsire cut in alabaster?

      Sleep when he wakes? and creep into the jaundice

90   By being peevish? I tell thee what, Antonio,—

      I love thee, and it is my love that speaks;—

      There are a sort of men, whose visages

      Do cream and mantle like a standing pond;

      And do a wilful stillness entertain,

95   With purpose to be dress'd in an opinion

      Of wisdom, gravity, profound conceit;

      As who should say, I am Sir Oracle,

      And, when I ope my lips, let no dog bark!

      O, my Antonio, I do know of these,

100   That therefore only are reputed wise,

      For saying nothing; who, I am very sure,

      If they should speak, would almost damn those ears

      Which, hearing them, would call their brothers, fools.

      I'll tell thee more of this another time:

105   But fish not with this melancholy bait,

      For this fool-gudgeon, this opinion.

      Come, good Lorenzo:— Fare ye well, awhile:

      I'll end my exhortation after dinner.

LORENZO: Well, we will leave you

110   then till dinner-time.

I must be one of these same dumb wise men,
For Gratiano never lets me speak.
GRATIANO: Well, keep me company but two years more,
Thou shalt not know the sound of thine own tongue.
115 ANTONIO: Farewell: I'll grow a talker for this gear.
GRATIANO: Thanks, i' faith; for silence is only commendable
In a neat's tongue dried, and a maid not vendible.†

[*Gratiano and Lorenzo exit.*]

ANTONIO: Is that any thing now?
BASSANIO: Gratiano speaks an infinite deal of nothing, more
120   than any man in all Venice: his reasons are as two grains
of wheat hid in two bushels of chaff; you shall seek all
day ere you find them; and when you have them they are
not worth the search.
ANTONIO: Well; tell me now, what lady is the same
125   To whom you swore a secret pilgrimage,
That you to-day promis'd to tell me of?
BASSANIO: 'Tis not unknown to you, Antonio,
How much I have disabled mine estate,
By something showing a more swelling port
130   Than my faint means would grant continuance:†
Nor do I now make moan to be abridg'd
From such a noble rate; but my chief care
Is to come fairly off from the great debts
Wherein my time, something too prodigal,
135   Hath left me gag'd. To you, Antonio,
I owe the most in money and in love;
And from your love I have a warranty
To unburthen all my plots and purposes,
How to get clear of all the debts I owe.
140 ANTONIO: I pray you, good Bassanio, let me know it;
And, if it stand, as you yourself still do,
Within the eye of honour, be assur'd,
My purse, my person, my extremest means,
Lie all unlock'd to your occasions.
145 BASSANIO: In my schooldays, when I had lost one shaft,
I shot his fellow of the self-same flight
The self-same way, with more advised watch,
To find the other forth; and by adventuring both
I oft found both: I urge this childhood proof,
150   Because what follows is pure innocence.
I owe you much; and, like a wilful youth,

That which I owe is lost: but if you please
To shoot another arrow that self way
Which you did shoot the first, I do not doubt,
155   As I will watch the aim, or to find both,
Or bring your latter hazard back again,
And thankfully rest debtor for the first.
ANTONIO: You know me well, and herein spend but time,
To wind about my love with circumstance;
160   And, out of doubt, you do me now more wrong
In making question of my uttermost,
Than if you had made waste of all I have.
Then do but say to me what I should do,
That in your knowledge may by me be done,
165   And I am prest unto it: therefore speak.
BASSANIO: In Belmont is a lady richly left,[4]
And she is fair, and, fairer than that word,
Of wondrous virtues. Sometimes from her eyes
I did receive fair speechless messages:
170   Her name is Portia; nothing undervalued
To Cato's daughter, Brutus' Portia.
Nor is the wide world ignorant of her worth;
For the four winds blow in from every coast
Renowned suitors, and her sunny locks
175   Hang on her temples like a golden fleece;
Which makes her seat of Belmont, Colchos' strand,[5]
And many Jasons† come in quest of her.
O, my Antonio! had I but the means
To hold a rival place with one of them,
180   I have a mind presages me such thrift,
That I should questionless be fortunate.
ANTONIO: Thou know'st that all my fortunes are at sea;
Neither have I money, nor commodity
To raise a present sum: therefore go forth.
185   Try what my credit can in Venice do;
That shall be rack'd, even to the uttermost,[6]
To furnish thee to Belmont, to fair Portia.
Go, presently inquire, and so will I,
Where money is; and I no question make,
190   To have it of my trust, or for my sake.

                                    Exeunt.

[4]*an heiress to large amounts of money*

→ reference to Jason (handwritten note)

[5]*the shores of Belmont*

[6]*"my credit will be stretched thinly"*

[SCENE II]
[Belmont]

Enter Portia with her waiting woman Nerissa.

PORTIA: By my troth,[1] Nerissa, my little body is a-weary of
this great world.

NERISSA: You would be, sweet madam, if your miseries were
in the same abundance as your good fortunes are; and yet,
5   for aught I see, they are as sick that surfeit with too much,
as they that starve with nothing. It is no mean happiness,
therefore, to be seated in the mean; superfluity comes
sooner by white hairs, but competency lives longer.

PORTIA: Good sentences, and well pronounced.

10 NERISSA: They would be better, if well followed.

PORTIA: If to do were as easy as to know what were good to
do, chapels had been churches, and poor men's cottages
princes' palaces. It is a good divine that follows his own
instructions: I can easier teach twenty what were good to
15   be done, than be one of the twenty to follow mine own
teaching. The brain may devise laws for the blood; but a
hot temper leaps o'er a cold decree: such a hare is madness the youth, to skip o'er the meshes of good counsel
the cripple. But this reasoning is not in the fashion to
20   choose me a husband:—O me, the word choose! I may
neither choose whom I would, nor refuse whom I dislike;
so is the will of a living daughter curbed by the will of a
dead father:—Is it not hard, Nerissa, that I cannot choose
one, nor refuse none?

25 NERISSA: Your father was ever virtuous; and holy men at their
death have good inspirations; therefore, the lottery that
he hath devised in these three chests, of gold, silver, and
lead, (whereof who chooses his meaning chooses you,)
will, no doubt, never be chosen by any rightly, but one
30   who you shall rightly love. But what warmth is there in
your affection towards any of these princely suitors that
are already come?

PORTIA: I pray thee, over-name them; and as thou namest
them I will describe them; and according to my descrip-
35   tion level at my affection.

NERISSA: First, there is the Neapolitan prince.

PORTIA: Ay, that's a colt, indeed, for he doth nothing but talk

---

[1]*truth*

of his horse; and he makes it a great appropriation to his own good parts that he can shoe him himself: I am much 40 afraid my lady his mother played false with a smith.

NERISSA: Then, is there the county Palatine.

PORITA: He doth nothing but frown; as who should say, An you will not have me, choose; he hears merry tales, and smiles not: I fear he will prove the weeping philosopher when he 45 grows old, being so full of unmannerly sadness in his youth. I had rather be married to a death's head with a bone in his mouth, than to either of these. God defend me from these two!

NERISSA: How say you by the French lord, Monsieur Le Bon?

50 PORTIA: God made him, and therefore let him pass for a man. In truth, I know it is a sin to be a mocker; but, he! why, he hath a horse better than the Neapolitan's; a better bad habit of frowning than the count Palatine: he is every man in no man; if a throstle[2] sing he falls straight a capering;[3] he will 55 fence with his own shadow: if I should marry him I should marry twenty husbands: If he would despise me I would forgive him; for if he love me to madness I shall never requite him.[4]

NERISSA: What say you then to Falconbridge, the young baron 60 of England?

PORTIA: You know I say nothing to him; for he understands not me, nor I him: he hath neither Latin, French, nor Italian; and you will come into the court, and swear that I have a poor pennyworth in the English. He is a proper man's pic-65 ture; but, alas! who can converse with a dumb show? How oddly he is suited! I think he bought his doublet[5] in Italy, his round hose[6] in France, his bonnet in Germany and his behaviour everywhere.

NERISSA: What think you of the Scottish lord, his neighbour?

70 PORTIA: That he hath a neighbourly charity in him; for he borrowed a box of the ear of the Englishman, and swore he would pay him again when he was able: I think the Frenchman became his surety, and sealed under for another.[†]

NERISSA: How like you the young German, the Duke of Saxony's 75 nephew?

PORTIA: Very vilely in the morning, when he is sober; and most vilely in the afternoon, when he is drunk: when he is best, he is a little worse than a man; and when he is worst, he is little better than a beast: and the worst fall that ever fell, I

[2]*bird*

[3]*dancing, frolicking*

[4]*"I shall never return his love."*

[5]*jacket*

[6]*stockings*

80   hope I shall make shift to go without him.

NERISSA: If he should offer to choose, and choose the right
casket, you should refuse to perform your father's will, if
you should refuse to accept him.

PORTIA: Therefore, for fear of the worst, I pray thee, set a deep

7the opposite

85   glass of Rhenish wine on the contrary[7] casket; for, if the
devil be within and that temptation without, I know he
will choose it. I will do anything, Nerissa, ere I will be
married to a sponge.

NERISSA: You need not fear, lady, the having any of these

90   lords: they have acquainted me with their determina-
tions: which is, indeed, to return to their home, and to

8courting, wooing;
romance

trouble you with no more suit;[8] unless you may be won
by some other sort than your father's imposition, depend-
ing on the caskets.

9pure

95 PORTIA: If I live to be as old as Sibylla† I will die as chaste[9] as
Diana,† unless I be obtained by the manner of my father's
will. I am glad this parcel of wooers are so reasonable;
for there is not one among them but I dote on his very
absence, and I pray God grant them a fair departure.

100 NERISSA: Do you not remember, lady, in your father's time,
a Venetian, a scholar and a soldier that came hither in
company of the Marquis of Montferrat?

PORTIA: Yes, yes, it was Bassanio; as I think, so was he
called.

105 NERISSA: True, madam; he, of all the men that ever my foolish
eyes looked upon, was the best deserving a fair lady.

PORTIA: I remember him well; and I remember him worthy
of thy praise.

Enter a Servingman.

How now! what news?

110 SERVINGMAN: The four strangers seek for you, madam, to take
their leave: and there is a forerunner come from a fifth,
the Prince of Morocco; who brings word, the prince, his
master, will be here to-night.

PORTIA: If I could bid the fifth welcome with so good a heart

115   as I can bid the other four farewell, I should be glad of
his approach: if he have the condition of a saint and the
complexion of a devil, I had rather he should shrive me
than wive me.† Come, Nerissa. Sirrah, go before; whiles
we shut the gate upon one wooer, another knocks at the

120   door.   *Exeunt.*

[SCENE III]
[Venice]

Enter Bassanio with Shylock the Jew.

SHYLOCK: Three thousand ducats,—well.

BASSANIO: Ay, sir, for three months.

SHYLOCK: For three months,—well.

BASSANIO: For the which, as I told you, Antonio shall be
5   bound.[1]

SHYLOCK: Antonio shall become bound,—well.

BASSANIO: May you stead[2] me? Will you pleasure me? Shall I
    know your answer?

SHYLOCK: Three thousand ducats, for three months, and Antonio
10   bound.

BASSANIO: Your answer to that.

SHYLOCK: Antonio is a good man.

BASSANIO: Have you heard any imputation to the contrary?

SHYLOCK: Ho! no, no, no, no;—my meaning in saying he is a
15   good man, is, to have you understand me that he is suffi-
    cient:[3] Yet his means are in supposition:[4] he hath an argosy[5]
    bound to Tripolis, another to the Indies; I understand more-
    over upon the Rialto,† he hath a third at Mexico, a fourth for
    England; and other ventures he hath, squander'd abroad. But
20   ships are but boards, sailors but men: there be land-rats and
    water-rats, land-thieves and water-thieves; I mean, pirates;
    and then, there is the peril of waters, winds, and rocks. The
    man is, notwithstanding, sufficient;—three thousand duc-
    ats;—I think I may take his bond.

25 BASSANIO: Be assured you may.

SHYLOCK: I will be assured I may; and that I may be assured, I
    will bethink me. May I speak with Antonio?

BASSANIO: If it please you to dine with us.

SHYLOCK: Yes, to smell pork; to eat of the habitation which your
30   prophet, the Nazarite,† conjured the devil into! I will buy
    with you, sell with you, talk with you, walk with you, and
    so following; but I will not eat with you, drink with you,
    nor pray with you.—What news on the Rialto?—Who is he
    comes here?

Enter Antonio.

[1] *"Antonio will be responsible for repaying the debt."*

[2] *help*

[3] *competent; trustworthy*

[4] *"risky money investments"*

[5] *a fleet of ships*

35   BASSANIO: This is Signior Antonio.

SHYLOCK: How like a fawning publican he looks!
      I hate him for he is a Christian:
      But more, for that, in low simplicity,
      He lends out money gratis,[6] and brings down
40   The rate of usance[7] here with us in Venice.
      If I can catch him once upon the hip,
      I will feed fat the ancient grudge I bear him.
      He hates our sacred nation; and he rails,
      Even there where merchants most do congregate,
45   On me, my bargains, and my well-won thrift,
      Which he calls interest. Cursed be my tribe
      If I forgive him!

BASSANIO: Shylock, do you hear?

SHYLOCK: I am debating of my present store:
50   And, by the near guess of my memory,
      I cannot instantly raise up the gross
      Of full three thousand ducats. What of that?
      Tubal, a wealthy Hebrew of my tribe,
      Will furnish me. But soft: how many months
55   Do you desire?—Rest you fair, good signior:
      Your worship was the last man in our mouths.[8]

ANTONIO: Shylock, albeit I neither lend nor borrow,
      By taking, nor by giving of excess,
      Yet, to supply the ripe wants of my friend,
60   I'll break a custom:—Is he yet possess'd
      How much you would?

SHYLOCK: Ay, ay, three thousand ducats.

ANTONIO: And for three months.

SHYLOCK: I had forgot;—three months. You told me so.
65   Well then, your bond; and, let me see. but hear you:
      Methought you said, you neither lend nor borrow,
      Upon advantage.

ANTONIO: I do never use it.

SHYLOCK: When Jacob graz'd his uncle Laban's sheep,
70   This Jacob from our holy Abram was
      (As his wise mother wrought in his behalf)
      The third possessor; ay, he was the third.

ANTONIO: And what of him? did he take interest?

SHYLOCK: No, not take interest; not, as you would say,
75   Directly interest: mark what Jacob did.
      When Laban and himself were compromis'd

---

[6]free, without interest

[7]interest

[8]"We were just talking about you."

That all the eanlings which were streak'd and pied[9]
Should fall, as Jacob's hire; the ewes, being rank,
In the end of autumn turned to the rams:
80   And when the work of generation was,
Between these woolly breeders, in the act,
The skilful shepherd pill'd me certain wands,
And, in the doing of the deed of kind,
He stuck them up before the fulsome ewes;
85   Who, then conceiving, did in eaning-time
Fall party-colour'd lambs, and those were Jacob's.
This was a way to thrive, and he was blest;
And thrift is blessing, if men steal it not.
ANTONIO: This was a venture,[10] sir, that Jacob serv'd for;
90   A thing not in his power to bring to pass,
But sway'd and fashion'd by the hand of Heaven.
Was this inserted to make interest good?
Or is your gold and silver ewes and rams?
SHYLOCK: I cannot tell; I make it breed as fast:
95   But note me, signior.
ANTONIO: Mark you this, Bassanio,
The devil can cite Scripture for his purpose.
An evil soul producing holy witness
Is like a villain with a smiling cheek;
100   A goodly apple rotten at the heart;
O, what a goodly outside falsehood hath!
SHYLOCK: Three thousand ducats;—'tis a good round sum.
Three months from twelve, then let me see; the rate.
ANTONIO: Well, Shylock, shall we be beholden to you?
105 SHYLOCK: Signior Antonio, many a time and oft,
In the Rialto you have rated me
About my moneys, and my usances:
Still have I borne it with a patient shrug,
For sufferance is the badge of all our tribe:
110   You call me,—misbeliever, cut-throat dog,
And spet upon my Jewish gaberdine,[11]
And all for use of that which is mine own.
Well then, it now appears you need my help:
Go to then: you come to me, and you say,
115   Shylock, we would have monies; you say so;
You, that did void your rheum[12] upon my beard,
And foot me, as you spurn a stranger cur
Over your threshold; monies is your suit.

[9] *patchy in color*

[10] *a risk, gamble*

[11] *clothing*

[12] *spit*

What should I say to you? Should I not say,

120   Hath a dog money? is it possible

A cur can lend three thousand ducats? or

Shall I bend low, and in a bondman's key,

With 'bated breath, and whispering humbleness,

Say this,—

125   'Fair sir, you spat on me on Wednesday last;

You spurn'd me such a day; another time

You call'd me—dog; and for these courtesies

I'll lend you thus much moneys?'

ANTONIO: I am as like to call thee so again,

130   To spit on thee again, to spurn thee too.

If thou wilt lend this money, lend it not

As to thy friends; (for when did friendship take

A breed for barren metal of his friend?)[13]

But lend it rather to thine enemy;

135   Who, if he break, thou mayst with better face

Exact the penalty.

SHYLOCK: Why, look you, how you storm!

I would be friends with you, and have your love,

Forget the shames that you have stain'd me with,

140   Supply your present wants, and take no doit

Of usance for my monies, and you'll not hear me:

This is kind I offer.

BASSANIO: This were kindness.

SHYLOCK: This kindness will I show:

145   Go with me to a notary, seal me there

Your single bond; and, in a merry sport,

If you repay me not on such a day,

In such a place, such sum, or sums, as are

Express'd in the condition, let the forfeit

150   Be nominated for an equal pound

Of your fair flesh, to be cut off and taken

In what part of your body pleaseth me.

ANTONIO: Content, in faith; I'll seal to such a bond,

And say there is much kindness in the Jew.

155 BASSANIO: You shall not seal to such a bond for me;

I'll rather dwell in my necessity.

ANTONIO: Why, fear not, man, I will not forfeit it;

Within these two months,—that's a month before

This bond expires,—I do expect return

160   Of thrice three times the value of this bond.

[13]*"a friend doesn't charge a friend interest"*

SHYLOCK: O father Abram, what these Christians are,
　　　Whose own hard dealings teaches them suspect
　　　The thoughts of others! Pray you, tell me this;
　　　If he should break his day, what should I gain
165　　By the exaction of the forfeiture?
　　　A pound of man's flesh, taken from a man,
　　　Is not so estimable, profitable neither,
　　　As flesh of muttons, beefs, or goats. I say,
　　　To buy his favour, I extend this friendship;
170　　If he will take it, so; if not, adieu;
　　　And, for my love, I pray you wrong me not.
ANTONIO: Yes, Shylock, I will seal unto this bond.
SHYLOCK: Then meet me forthwith at the notary's;
　　　Give him direction for this merry bond,
175　　And I will go and purse the ducats straight;
　　　See to my house, left in the fearful guard
　　　Of an unthrifty knave; and presently
　　　I will be with you.   *Exit.*
ANTONIO: Hie thee, gentle Jew.
180　　This Hebrew will turn Christian; he grows kind.
BASSANIO: I like not fair terms and a villain's mind.
ANTONIO: Come on; in this there can be no dismay,
　　　My ships come home a month before the day.

                                                    Exeunt.

ACT II

ACT II

[SCENE I]
[Belmont]

Enter Morocco a tawny Moor all in white, and three or four follow-
ers accordingly, with Portia, Nerissa, and their traine.

Flour[ish] cornets.

MOROCCO: Mislike me not for my complexion,
 The shadowed livery of the burnish'd sun,
 To whom I am a neighbour, and near bred.
 Bring me the fairest creature northward born,
5 Where Phoebus' fire† scarce thaws the icicles,
 And let us make incision for your love,
 To prove whose blood is reddest, his, or mine.
 I tell thee, lady, this aspect of mine
 Hath fear'd the valiant; by my love, I swear,
10 The best-regarded virgins of our clime[1]   [1]*climate*
 Have lov'd it too: I would not change this hue,[2] [2]*color, shade*
 Except to steal your thoughts, my gentle queen.
PORTIA: In terms of choice I am not solely led
 By nice direction of a maiden's eyes:
15 Besides, the lottery of my destiny
 Bars me the right of voluntary choosing:
 But, if my father had not scanted[3] me,   [3]*restricted*
 And hedg'd[4] me by his wit, to yield myself   [4]*enclosed*
 His wife, who wins me by that means I told you,
20 Yourself, renowned prince, then stood as fair
 As any comer I have look'd on yet,
 For my affection.
MOROCCO: Even for that I thank you;
 Therefore, I pray you, lead me to the caskets,
25 To try my fortune. By this scimitar,[5]—   [5]*sword*
 That slew the Sophy,† and a Persian prince,
 That won three fields of Sultan Solyman,†—

I would o'erstare the sternest eyes that look,
Outbrave the heart most daring on the earth,
30 Pluck the young sucking cubs from the she-bear,
Yea, mock the lion when he roars for prey,
To win thee, lady. But, alas the while!
If Hercules and Lichas[†] play at dice
Which is the better man, the greater throw
35 May turn by fortune from the weaker hand:
So is Alcides[†] beaten by his page;
And so may I, blind fortune leading me,
Miss that which one unworthier may attain,
And die with grieving.
40 PORTIA: You must take your chance;
And either not attempt to choose at all,
Or swear, before you choose,—if you choose wrong,
Never to speak to lady afterward
In way of marriage; therefore be advis'd.
45 MOROCCO: Nor will not; come, bring me unto my chance.
PORTIA: First, forward to the temple; after dinner
Your hazard shall be made.[6]
MOROCCO: Good fortune, then!   *Cornets.*
To make me bless'd, or cursed'st among men.
                                                Exeunt.

arrogant (handwritten)

[SCENE II]
[Venice]

Enter the clown [Launcelot] alone.

[LAUNCELOT:] Certainly, my conscience will serve me to run
from this Jew, my master. The fiend is at mine elbow, and
tempts me; saying to me,—Gobbo, Launcelot Gobbo,
good Launcelot, or good Gobbo, or good Launcelot
5   Gobbo, use your legs, take the start, run away.—My
conscience says, no; take heed, honest Launcelot; take
heed, honest Gobbo; or, (as aforesaid) honest Launcelot
Gobbo; do not run: scorn running with thy heels: well,
the most courageous fiend bids me pack; Via![1] says the
10 fiend; away! says the fiend, for the heavens rouse up a
brave mind, says the fiend, and run. Well, my conscience,
hanging about the neck of my heart, says very wisely to
me,—my honest friend Launcelot, being an honest man's

Launcelot – servant of Snylock (handwritten)

son: or rather an honest woman's son;—for, indeed, my
15   father did something smack,[2] something grow to, he had a
kind of taste;—well, my conscience says, Launcelot, budge
not: budge, says the fiend; budge not, says my conscience:
Conscience, say I, you counsel well; fiend, say I, you counsel well: to be ruled by my conscience, I should stay with
20   the Jew my master, who, (God bless the mark!) is a kind of
devil; and to run away from the Jew, I should be ruled by
the fiend, who, saving your reverence, is the devil himself.
Certainly, the Jew is the very devil incarnation: and, in my
conscience, my conscience is but a kind of hard conscience,
25   to offer to counsel me to stay with the Jew: the fiend gives
the more friendly counsel: I will run, fiend; my heels are at
your command, I will run.

Enter old Gobbo with a Basket.

GOBBO: Master, young man, you; I pray you, which is the way
to master Jew's?
30 LAUNCELOT: O heavens, this is my true-begotten father! who,
being more than sand-blind, high-gravel blind, knows me
not: I will try confusions with him.
GOBBO: Master, young gentleman, I pray you which is the way
to master Jew's?
35 LAUNCELOT: Turn up on your right hand at the next turning,
but, at the next turning of all, on your left; marry, at the very
next turning, turn of no hand, but turn down indirectly to
the Jew's house.
GOBBO: By God's sonties, 'twill be a hard way to hit. Can you
40   tell me whether one Launcelot, that dwells with him, dwell
with him, or no?
LAUNCELOT: Talk you of young Master Launcelot?—Mark me
now—now will I raise the waters.—Talk you of young master Launcelot?
45 GOBBO: No master, sir, but a poor man's son: his father, though
I say it, is an honest exceeding poor man, and, God be
thanked, well to live.
LAUNCELOT: Well, let his father be what a will, we talk of young
master Launcelot.
50 GOBBO: Your worship's friend and Launcelot, sir.
LAUNCELOT: But I pray you ergo, old man, ergo, I beseech you,
talk you of young master Launcelot.

[2] *taste*

GOBBO: Of Launcelot, an't please your mastership.

LAUNCELOT: Ergo, master Launcelot; talk not of Master
55   Launcelot, father; for the young gentleman (according
       to fates and destinies, and such odd sayings, the sis-
       ters three,† and such branches of learning) is, indeed,
       deceased; or, as you would say in plain terms, gone to
       heaven.

60 GOBBO: Marry, God forbid! the boy was the very staff of my
       age, my very prop.

LAUNCELOT: Do I look like a cudgel, or a hovel-post, a staff,
       or a prop? Do you know me, father?

GOBBO: Alack the day, I know you not, young gentleman:
65   but, I pray you tell me, is my boy (God rest his soul!)
       alive or dead?

LAUNCELOT: Do you not know me, father?

GOBBO: Alack, sir, I am sand-blind, I know you not.

LAUNCELOT: Nay, indeed, if you had your eyes you might fail
70   of the knowing me: it is a wise father that knows his own
       child. Well, old man, I will tell you news of your son: give
       me your blessing: truth will come to light; murder can-
       not be hid long; a man's son may; but, in the end, truth
       will out.

75 GOBBO: Pray you, sir, stand up; I am sure you are not
       Launcelot, my boy.

LAUNCELOT: Pray you, let's have no more fooling about it, but
       give me your blessing; I am Launcelot, your boy that was,
       your son that is, your child that shall be.

80 GOBBO: I cannot think you are my son.

LAUNCELOT: I know not what I shall think of that: but I am
       Launcelot, the Jew's man; and I am sure Margery, your
       wife, is my mother.

GOBBO: Her name is Margery, indeed: I'll be sworn, if thou
85   be Launcelot, thou art mine own flesh and blood. Lord
       worshipped might he be! what a beard hast thou got!
       thou hast got more hair on thy chin than Dobbin my
       phill-horse has on his tail.

LAUNCELOT: It should seem then, that Dobbin's tail grows
90   backward: I am sure he had more hair of his tail, than I
       have of my face, when I last saw him.

GOBBO: Lord, how art thou changed! How dost thou and thy
       master agree? I have brought him a present. How 'gree
       you now?

[handwritten margin note: Foreshadows: person who answers riddle correctly must satisfy Portia's father's standard.]

95 LAUNCELOT: Well, well; but, for mine own part, as I have set up
     my rest to run away, so I will not rest till I have run some
     ground. My master's a very Jew. Give him a present! give him
     a halter: I am famished in his service; you may tell every fin-
     ger I have with my ribs. Father, I am glad you are come: give
100 me your present to one master Bassanio, who, indeed, gives
     rare new liveries; if I serve not him, I will run as far as God
     has any ground.—O rare fortune! here comes the man;—to
     him, father; for I am a Jew if I serve the Jew any longer.

Enter Bassanio with a follower or two [one of them Leonardo.]

     BASSANIO: You may do so:—but let it be so hasted, that supper
105 be ready at the farthest by five of the clock. See these letters
     delivered; put the liveries to making; and desire Gratiano to
     come anon to my lodging.
     LAUNCELOT: To him, father.
     GOBBO: God bless your worship!
110 BASSANIO: Gramercy! wouldst thou aught with me?
     GOBBO: Here's my son, sir, a poor boy,—
     LAUNCELOT: Not a poor boy, sir, but the rich Jew's man; that
     would, sir, as my father shall specify,—
     GOBBO: He hath a great infection,[3] sir, as one would say, to
115 serve,—
     LAUNCELOT: Indeed, the short and the long is, I serve the Jew,
     and have a desire, as my father shall specify,—
     GOBBO: His master and he (saving your worship's reverence) are
     scarce cater-cousins:—
120 LAUNCELOT: To be brief, the very truth is, that the Jew having
     done me wrong, doth cause me, as my father, being I hope
     an old man, shall frutify unto you, —
     GOBBO: I have here a dish of doves,† that I would bestow upon
     your worship; and my suit is,—
125 LAUNCELOT: In very brief, the suit is impertinent[4] to myself,
     as your worship shall know by this honest old man; and,
     though I say it, though old man, yet, poor man, my father.
     BASSANIO: One speak for both:—what would you?
     LAUNCELOT: Serve you, sir.
130 GOBBO: That is the very defect[5] of the matter, sir.
     BASSANIO: I know thee well; thou hast obtain'd thy suit:[6]
     Shylock, thy master, spoke with me this day,
     And hath preferr'd thee, if it be preferment

[3]*old Gobbo's mistake for affection†*

[4]*Lancelot's mistake for pertinent*

[5]*Gobbo's mistake for effect*

[6]*"You will get what you ask for."*

To leave a rich Jew's service, to become

135   The follower of so poor a gentleman.

[LAUNCELOT:] The old proverb is very well parted between
my master Shylock and you, sir; you have the grace of
God, sir, and he hath enough.

BASSANIO: Thou speak'st it well. Go, father, with thy son:—

140   Take leave of thy old master, and inquire
My lodging out:—Give him a livery
More guarded than his fellows: see it done.

[LAUNCELOT:] Father, in:—I cannot get a service, no!—I have
ne'er a tongue in my head![7]—well! If any man in Italy

145   have a fairer table, which doth offer to swear upon a
book, I shall have good fortune! Go to, here's a simple
line of life! here's a small trifle of wives: alas, fifteen wives
is nothing; aleven widows and nine maids, is a simple
coming-in for one man: and then, to 'scape drowning

150   thrice; and to be in peril of my life with the edge of a
feather bed; here are simple 'scapes! Well, if fortune be a
woman, she's a good wench for this gear.—Father, come.
I'll take my leave of the Jew in the twinkling of an eye.[†]

Exit Clown.

BASSANIO: I pray thee, good Leonardo, think on this.

155   These things being bought, and orderly bestow'd,
Return in haste, for I do feast to-night
My best-esteem'd acquaintance: hie thee Go.

LEONARDO: My best endeavours shall be done herein.

Exit Leonardo.

Enter Gratiano.

GRATIANO: Where's your master?

160 LEONARDO: Yonder, sir, he walks.

GRATIANO: Signior Bassanio,—

BASSANIO: Gratiano!

GRATIANO: I have a suit to you.

BASSANIO: You have obtain'd it.

165 GRATIANO: You must not deny me. I must go with you to
Belmont.

BASSANIO: Why, then you must.—But hear thee, Gratiano;
Thou art too wild, too rude and bold of voice;
Parts, that become thee happily enough,

[7] *"I am unable to speak for myself."*

170   And in such eyes as ours appear not faults;
        But where thou art not known, why, there they show
        Something too liberal: pray thee, take pain
        To allay with some cold drops of modesty,
        Thy skipping spirit; lest, through thy wild behavior,
175   I be misconster'd in the place I go to,
        And lose my hopes.
GRATIANO: Signior Bassanio, hear me:
        If I do not put on a sober habit,[8]
        Talk with respect, and swear but now and then,
180   Wear prayer-books in my pocket, look demurely;
        Nay more, while grace is saying, hood mine eyes
        Thus with my hat, and sigh, and say Amen;
        Use all the observance of civility,
        Like one well studied in a sad ostent[9]
185   To please his grandam,—never trust me more.
BASSANIO: Well, we shall see your bearing.
GRATIANO: Nay, but I bar to-night; you shall not gage me
        By what we do to-night.
BASSANIO: No, that were pity;
190   I would entreat you rather to put on
        Your boldest suit of mirth, for we have friends
        That purpose merriment. But fare you well,
        I have some business.
GRATIANO: And I must to Lorenzo and the rest;
195   But we will visit you at supper-time.

                                        Exeunt.

[8]*"put on modest clothes"*

[9]*grave appearance*

[SCENE III]
[Venice]

Enter Jessica and [Launcelot] the Clown.

JESSICA: I am sorry thou wilt leave my father so;
        Our house is hell, and thou, a merry devil,
        Didst rob it of some taste of tediousness:
        But fare thee well: there is a ducat for thee.
5   And, Launcelot, soon at supper shalt thou see
        Lorenzo, who is thy new master's guest:
        Give him this letter; do it secretly,
        And so farewell; I would not have my father

See me in talk with thee.

10 [LAUNCELOT:] Adieu!—tears exhibit[1] my tongue. Most beautiful pagan,—most sweet Jew! If a Christian did not play the knave and get thee, I am much deceived. But, adieu! these foolish drops do something drown my manly spirit: adieu! *Exit.*

15 JESSICA: Farewell, good Launcelot.
Alack, what heinous sin is it in me,
To be asham'd to be my father's child!
But though I am a daughter to his blood,
I am not to his manners: O Lorenzo!
20 If thou keep promise, I shall end this strife;
Become a Christian, and thy loving wife.

Exit.

[SCENE IV]
[Venice]

Enter Gratiano, Lorenzo, Salerio, and Solanio.

LORENZO: Nay, we will slink away in supper-time,
Disguise us at my lodging, and return,
All in an hour.
GRATIANO: We have not made good preparation.
5 SALERIO: We have not spoke us yet of torchbearers.
SOLANIO: 'Tis vile, unless it may be quaintly ordered,[1]
And better, in my mind, not undertook.
LORENZO: 'Tis now but four o'clock; we have two hours,
To furnish us.—
10   Friend Launcelot, what's the news?

Enter Launcelot, with a letter.

LAUNCELOT: An[2] it shall please you to break up this, it shall seem to signify.
LORENZO: I know the hand: in faith, 'tis a fair hand;
And whiter than the paper it writ on,
15 Is the fair hand that writ.
GRATIANO: Love-news, in faith.
LAUNCELOT: By your leave, sir.
LORENZO: Whither goest thou?

LAUNCELOT: Marry, sir, to bid my old master the Jew to sup
20   to-night with my new master the Christian.
LORENZO: Hold here, take this.—Tell gentle Jessica,
        I will not fail her.—Speak it privately.
        Go. Gentlemen,will you prepare you for this masque
            to-night?
25   I am provided of a torch-bearer.   *Exit Clown.*
SALERIO: Ay, marry, I'll be gone about it straight.
SOLANIO: And so will I.
LORENZO: Meet me and Gratiano,
        At Gratiano's lodging some hour hence.
30 SALERIO: 'Tis good we do so.
                              Exit [Salerio and Solanio]
GRATIANO: Was not that letter from fair Jessica?
LORENZO: I must needs tell thee all. She hath directed
        How I shall take her from her father's house;
        What gold and jewels she is furnish'd with;
35   What page's suit she hath in readiness.
        If e'er the Jew her father come to heaven,
        It will be for his gentle daughter's sake:
        And never dare misfortune cross her foot,
        Unless she do it under this excuse,—
40   That she is issue to a faithless Jew.
        Come, go with me; peruse this as thou goest:
        Fair Jessica shall be my torchbearer.
                                        Exit.

[SCENE V]
[Venice]

Enter [Shylock,] Jew, his man that was the Clown [Launcelot].

[SHYLOCK:] Well, thou shalt see, thy eyes shall be thy judge,
        The difference of old Shylock and Bassanio:—
        What, Jessica!—thou shalt not gormandise,
        As thou hast done with me;—What, Jessica!—
5   And sleep, and snore, and rend apparel out;—
        Why, Jessica, I say!
[LAUNCELOT:]   Why, Jessica!
SHYLOCK: Who bids thee call? I do not bid thee call.

[LAUNCELOT:] Your worship was wont to tell me, I could do
10   nothing without bidding.

Enter Jessica.

JESSICA: Call you? What is your will?
SHYLOCK: I am bid forth to supper, Jessica:
     There are my keys.—But wherefore should I go?
     I am not bid for love; they flatter me:
15   But yet I'll go in hate, to feed upon
     The prodigal Christian.—Jessica, my girl,
     Look to my house.—I am right loath to go;
     There is some ill a-brewing towards my rest,
     For I did dream of money-bags to-night.
20 [LAUNCELOT:] I beseech you, sir, go; my young master doth
     expect your reproach.[1]
SHYLOCK: So do I, his.
[LAUNCELOT:] And they have conspired together,—I will not
     say, you shall see a masque; but if you do, then it was
25   not for nothing that my nose fell a-bleeding on Black-
     Monday† last, at six o'clock i' the morning, falling out
     that year on Ash-Wednesday was four year in the after-
     noon.
SHYLOCK: What! are there masques? Hear you me, Jessica:
30   Lock up my doors; and when you hear the drum,
     And the vile squealing of the wry-neck'd[2] fife,
     Clamber not you up to the casements[3] then,
     Nor thrust your head into the public street,
     To gaze on Christian fools with varnish'd faces:
35   But stop my house's ears, I mean my casements;
     Let not the sound of shallow foppery enter
     My sober house.—By Jacob's staff I swear,
     I have no mind of feasting forth to-night:
     But I will go.—Go you before me, sirrah;
40   Say, I will come.
[LAUNCELOT:]   I will go before, sir.—
     Mistress, look out at window for all this;
     There will come a Christian by,
     Will be worth a Jewess'† eye.
45 SHYLOCK: What says that fool of Hagar's offspring;† ha?
JESSICA: His words were, Farewell mistress; nothing else.
SHYLOCK: The patch is kind enough; but a huge feeder,

[1]*approach*

[2]*crooked-necked*

[3]*windows*

Snail-slow in profit, and he sleeps by day
More than the wild cat: drones hive not with me,[4†]
50   Therefore I part with him; and part with him
To one, that I would have him help to waste
His borrow'd purse.—Well, Jessica, go in;
Perhaps, I will return immediately;
Do as I bid you, shut doors after you:
55   Fast bind, fast find;
A proverb never stale in thrifty mind.   *Exit.*
JESSICA: Farewell; and if my fortune be not cross'd,
I have a father, you a daughter, lost.   *Exit.*

[4] *"Lazy people will not live with me."*

[SCENE VI]

Enter the maskers, Gratiano and Salerio.

GRATIANO: This is the pent-house, under which Lorenzo
Desir'd us to make stand.
SALERIO: His hour is almost past.
GRATIANO: And it is marvel he out-dwells his hour,
5   For lovers ever run before the clock.
SALERIO: O, ten times faster Venus' pigeons[†] fly
To seal love's bonds new-made, than they are wont
To keep obliged faith[1] unforfeited!
GRATIANO: That ever holds: who riseth from a feast
10   With that keen appetite that he sits down?
Where is the horse that doth untread again,
His tedious measures with the unbated fire,
That he did pace them first? All things that are,
Are with more spirit chased than enjoy'd.
15   How like a younger,[2] or a prodigal,[†]
The scarfed bark[3] puts from her native bay,
Hugg'd and embraced by the strumpet[4] wind!

[1] *a promise to marry*

[2] *younger son*

[3] *a decorated ship*

[4] *a promiscuous woman*

Enter Lorenzo.
How like a prodigal doth she return;
With over-weather'd ribs, and ragged sails,
20   Lean, rent, and beggar'd by the strumpet wind!
SALERIO: Here comes Lorenzo;—more of this hereafter.
LORENZO: Sweet friends, your patience for my long abode:
Not I, but my affairs, have made you wait:

When you shall please to play the thieves for wives,
25   I'll watch as long for you then.—Approach;
Here dwells my father Jew.—Ho! who's within?

[Enter] Jessica above.

JESSICA: Who are you? Tell me, for more certainty,
Albeit I'll swear that I do know your tongue.
LORENZO: Lorenzo, and thy love.
30 JESSICA: Lorenzo, certain; and my love, indeed;
For who love I so much? And now, who knows
But you, Lorenzo, whether I am yours?
LORENZO: Heaven, and thy thoughts, are witness that thou
art.
35 JESSICA: Here, catch this casket; it is worth the pains.
I am glad 'tis night, you do not look on me,
For I am much asham'd of my exchange:
But love is blind, and lovers cannot see
The pretty follies that themselves commit;
40   For if they could, Cupid† himself would blush,
To see me thus transformed to a boy.
LORENZO: Descend, for you must be my torchbearer.
JESSICA: What, must I hold a candle to my shames?
They in themselves, good-sooth, are too-too light.
45   Why, 'tis an office of discovery, love;
And I should be obscur'd.
LORENZO: So are you, sweet,

5clothing

Even in the lovely garnish[5] of a boy.
But come at once;
50   For the close night doth play the run-away,
And we are stay'd for at Bassanio's feast.
JESSICA: I will make fast the doors, and gild myself
With some more ducats, and be with you straight.
                                 [Exit above]
GRATIANO: Now, by my hood, a Gentile and no Jew.

6Indeed

55 LORENZO: Beshrew[6] me, but I love her heartily:
For she is wise, if I can judge of her;
And fair she is, if that mine eyes be true;
And true she is, as she hath prov'd herself;
And therefore, like herself, wise, fair, and true,
60   Shall she be placed in my constant soul.

Enter Jessica, [below].
        What, art thou come?—On, gentlemen, away;
        Our masquing mates by this time for us stay.
                                        Exit [with Jessica and Salerio]

Enter Antonio

ANTONIO: Who's there?
GRATIANO: Signior Antonio!
65 ANTONIO: Fie, fie, Gratiano! where are all the rest?
        'Tis nine o'clock, our friends all stay for you:
        No masque to-night, the wind is come about;
        Bassanio presently will go aboard:
        I have sent twenty out to seek for you.
70 GRATIANO: I am glad on't; I desire no more delight,
        Than to be under sail and gone to-night.
                                        Exeunt.

[SCENE VII]
[Belmont]

Enter Portia with [the Prince of] Morocco, and both their trains.

PORTIA: Go, draw aside the curtains, and discover
        The several caskets to this noble prince:—
        Now make your choice.
MOROCCO: The first, of gold, who this inscription bears:
5   *Who chooseth me, shall gain what many men desire.*
        The second, silver, which this promise carries:
        Who chooseth me, shall get as much as he deserves.
        This third, dull lead, with warning all as blunt:
        Who chooseth me, must give and hazard all he hath.
10   How shall I know if I do choose the right?
PORTIA: The one of them contains my picture, prince;
        If you choose that, then I am yours withal.
MOROCCO: Some god direct my judgment! Let me see.
        I will survey the inscriptions back again:
15   What says this leaden casket:
        Who chooseth me, must give and hazard all he hath.
        Must give—For what? for lead? hazard for lead?

[1]something worth-
less

20   This casket threatens: Men that hazard all
      Do it in hope of fair advantages:
      A golden mind stoops not to shows of dross;[1]
      I'll then nor give, nor hazard, aught for lead.
      What says the silver, with her virgin hue?
      Who chooseth me, shall get as much as he deserves.
      As much as he deserves?—Pause there, Morocco,
25   And weigh thy value with an even hand:
      If thou be'st rated by thy estimation,[2]

[2]value, worth

      Thou dost deserve enough; and yet enough
      May not extend so far as to the lady:
      And yet to be afeard of my deserving,
30   Were but a weak disabling of myself.
      As much as I deserve!—Why, that's the lady:
      I do in birth deserve her, and in fortunes,
      In graces, and in qualities of breeding;
      But more than these, in love I do deserve.
35   What if I strayed no further, but chose here?—
      Let's see once more this saying grav'd in gold:
      Who chooseth me, shall gain what many men desire.
      Why, that's the lady: all the world desires her:
      From the four corners of the earth they come,
40   To kiss this shrine, this mortal, breathing, saint.
      The Hyrcanian deserts and the vasty wilds
      Of wide Arabia, are as through-fares now,
      For princes to come view fair Portia:
      The watery kingdom, whose ambitious head

[3]obstacle

45   Spets in the face of heaven, is no bar[3]
      To stop the foreign spirits; but they come,
      As o'er a brook, to see fair Portia.
      One of these three contains her heavenly picture.
      Is't like that lead contains her? 'Twere damnation
50   To think so base a thought: it were too gross
      To rib her cerecloth in the obscure grave.
      Or shall I think in silver she's immur'd,
      Being ten times undervalued to tried gold?
      O sinful thought! Never so rich a gem
55   Was set in worse than gold. They have in England,
      A coin that bears the figure of an angel,
      Stamped in gold; but that's insculp'd upon;
      But here an angel in a golden bed
      Lies all within.—Deliver me the key;

60   Here do I choose, and thrive I as I may!
     PORTIA: There, take it, prince, and if my form lie there,
          Then I am yours.   [*He unlocks the golden casket*]
     MOROCCO: O hell! what have we here?
          A carrion[4] Death, within whose empty eye
65   There is a written scroll? I'll read the writing.
          [*Reads*]

> All that glisters is not gold,
> Often have you heard that told:
> Many a man his life hath sold,
> But my outside to behold:
70 > Gilded[5] tombs do worms enfold.
> Had you been as wise as bold,
> Young in limbs, in judgment old,
> Your answer had not been inscroll'd:
> Fare you well; your suit is cold.

75   Cold, indeed; and labour lost:
          Then, farewell heat; and welcome frost.—
          Portia, adieu! I have too griev'd a heart
          To take a tedious leave. Thus losers part.

                                                        Exit.

     PORTIA: A gentle riddance:—Draw the curtains, go;—
80   Let all of his complexion choose me so.[6]

                                                        Exeunt.

[SCENE VIII]
[Venice]

Enter Salerio and Solanio.

     SALERIO: Why, man, I saw Bassanio under sail;
          With him is Gratiano gone along;
          And in their ship, I am sure, Lorenzo is not.
     SOLANIO: The villain Jew with outcries rais'd the duke;
5   Who went with him to search Bassanio's ship.
     SALERIO: He came too late, the ship was under sail:
          But there the duke was given to understand,
          That in a gondola were seen together
          Lorenzo and his amorous Jessica;
10   Besides, Antonio certified the duke,
          They were not with Bassanio in his ship.

[4]skeleton

[5]Golden

[6]"Let all those just like him make the same choice."

SOLANIO: I never heard a passion so confus'd,
So strange, outrageous, and so variable,
As the dog Jew did utter in the streets:
15   My daughter!—O my ducats!—O my daughter!
Fled with a Christian?—O my Christian ducats!—
Justice! the law! my ducats, and my daughter!
A sealed bag, two sealed bags of ducats,
Of double ducats, stol'n from me by my daughter!
20   And jewels; two stones, two rich and precious stones,
Stol'n by my daughter!—Justice! find the girl!
She hath the stones upon her, and the ducats!
SALERIO: Why, all the boys in Venice follow him
Crying,—'His stones, his daughter, and his ducats.'
25 SOLANIO: Let good Antonio look he keep his day,
Or he shall pay for this.
SALERIO: Marry, well remember'd:
I reason'd with a Frenchman yesterday,
Who told me,—in the narrow seas that part
30   The French and English, there miscarried
A vessel of our country, richly fraught:
I thought upon Antonio when he told me,
And wish'd in silence that it were not his.
SOLANIO: You were best to tell Antonio what you hear;
35   Yet do not suddenly, for it may grieve him.
SALERIO: A kinder gentleman treads not the earth.
I saw Bassanio and Antonio part:
Bassanio told him, he would make some speed
Of his return; he answer'd—Do not so,
40   Slubber not¹ business for my sake, Bassanio,
But stay the very riping of the time;²
And for the Jew's bond, which he hath of me,
Let it not enter in your mind of love:
Be merry; and employ your chiefest thoughts
45   To courtship, and such fair ostents³ of love,
As shall conveniently become you there:
And even there, his eye being big with tears,
Turning his face, he put his hand behind him,
And, with affection wondrous sensible,
50   He wrung Bassanio's hand, and so they parted.
SOLANIO: I think he only loves the world for him.
I pray thee, let us go and find him out,

¹"don't do it poorly"

²"stay as long as you need"

³appearances

And quicken his embraced heaviness,
With some delight or other.
55 SALERIO: Do we so.

                                              Exeunt.

[SCENE IX]
[Belmont]

Enter Nerissa and a servitor.

NERISSA: Quick, quick, I pray thee, draw the curtain straight;
    The Prince of Arragon hath ta'en his oath,
    And comes to his election presently.

*Enter [the Prince of] Arragon, his train, and Portia. Flourish of
cornets.*

PORTIA: Behold, there stand the caskets, noble prince;
5   If you choose that wherein I am contain'd,
    Straight shall our nuptial rites be solemniz'd;
    But if you fail, without more speech, my lord,
    You must be gone from hence immediately.
ARRAGON: I am enjoin'd by oath to observe three things:
10   First, never to unfold to any one,
    Which casket 'twas I chose; next, if I fail
    Of the right casket, never in my life
    To woo a maid in way of marriage; Lastly,
    If I do fail in fortune of my choice,
15   Immediately to leave you, and be gone.
PORTIA: To these injunctions every one doth swear,
    That comes to hazard for my worthless self.
ARRAGON: And so have I address'd me: Fortune now
    To my heart's hope!—Gold; silver; and base lead.
20   *Who chooseth me, must give and hazard all he hath.*
    You shall look fairer, ere I give, or hazard.
    What says the golden chest? ha! let me see:
    Who chooseth me, shall gain what many men desire.
    What many men desire.—that many may be meant
25   By the fool multitude, that choose by show,
    Not learning more than the fond eye doth teach;

Which pries not to th' interior, but, like the martlet,
Builds in the weather on the outward wall,
Even in the force and road of casualty.
30 I will not choose what many men desire,
Because I will not jump with common spirits,
And rank me with the barbarous multitudes.
Why, then to thee, thou silver treasure-house;
Tell me once more what title thou dost bear:
35 *Who chooseth me, shall get as much as he deserves.*
And well said too. for who shall go about

1cheat

To cozen¹ fortune, and be honourable
Without the stamp of merit! Let none presume

2"Don't let anyone presume to have an undeserved worth."

To wear an undeserved dignity:²
40 O, that estates, degrees, and offices,
Were not deriv'd corruptly! and that clear honour
Were purchas'd by the merit of the wearer!
How many then should cover that stand bare!
How many be commanded that command!

3collected

45 How much low peasantry would then be glean'd³
From the true seed of honour! and how much honour
Pick'd from the chaff and ruin of the times,
To be new varnish'd! Well, but to my choice:
Who chooseth me, shall get as much as he deserves.

4"I will assume I am deserving."

50 I will assume desert:⁴—Give me a key for this,
And instantly unlock my fortunes here.
                              [*He opens the silver casket*]
PORTIA: Too long a pause for that which you find there.
ARRAGON: What's here? the portrait of a blinking idiot,
    Presenting me a schedule! I will read it.
55 How much unlike art thou to Portia!
    How much unlike my hopes and my deservings!
    Who chooseth me, shall have as much as he deserves.
    Did I deserve no more than a fool's head?
    Is that my prize? are my deserts no better?
60 PORTIA: To offend, and judge, are distinct offices,
    And of opposed natures.⁵
ARRAGON: What is here?
    The fire seven times tried this;
    Seven times tried that judgment is,
65 *That did never choose amiss:*
    Some there be that shadows kiss,
    Such have but a shadow's bliss:

5"Criticizing while being judged are two distinct matters that work against each other"; the offender should not judhe his own case.

> There be fools alive, iwis,[6]
> Silver'd o'er; and so was this.
> 70 Take what wife you will to bed,
> I will ever be your head:
> So be gone: you are sped.[7]

Still more fool I shall appear,
By the time I linger here:
75 With one fool's head I came to woo,
But I go away with two.
Sweet, adieu! I'll keep my oath,
Patiently to bear my wroth.[8]

PORTIA: Thus hath the candle sing'd the moth.
80 O these deliberate fools! when they do choose,
They have the wisdom by their wit to lose.

NERISSA: The ancient saying is no heresy;—
Hanging and wiving goes by destiny.[9]

PORTIA: Come, draw the curtain, Nerissa.

Enter Messenger.

85 MESSENGER: Where is my lady?

PORTIA: Here; what would my lord?[10]

MESSENGER: Madam, there is alighted at your gate
A young Venetian, one that comes before
To signify the approaching of his lord;
90 From whom he bringeth sensible regreets;[11]
To wit,[12] (besides commends and courteous breath),
Gifts of rich value; Yet I have not seen
So likely an ambassador of love:
A day in April never came so sweet,
95 To show how costly summer was at hand,
As this fore-spurrer[13] comes before his lord.

PORTIA: No more, I pray thee; I am half afeard,
Thou wilt say anon he is some kin to thee,
Thou spend'st such high-day wit in praising him.
100 Come, come, Nerissa; for I long to see
Quick Cupid's post that comes so mannerly.

NERISSA: Bassanio, lord Love, if thy will it be.

Exeunts.

[6]*certainly*

[7]*out of luck*

[8]*sorrow*

[9]*"...getting a wife depends on destiny."*

[10]*"What is it, sir?"*

[11]*gifts and greetings*

[12]*That is*

[13]*messenger*

ACT III

[SCENE I]
[Venice]

[Enter Solanio and Salerio]

SOLANIO: Now, what news on the Rialto?
SALERIO: Why, yet it lives there unchecked that Antonio hath
    a ship of rich lading wrack'd on the narrow seas,—the
    Goodwins, I think they call the place; a very dangerous flat,
5   and fatal, where the carcasses of many a tall ship lie buried,
    as they say, if my gossip report, be an honest woman of her
    word.
SOLANIO: I would she were as lying a gossip in that, as ever
    knapped¹ ginger, or made her neighbours believe she wept
10   for the death of a third husband. But it is true,—without
    any slips of prolixity,² or crossing the plain highway of
    talk,—that the good Antonio, the honest Antonio,—O that
    I had a title good enough to keep his name company!—
SALERIO: Come, the full stop.
15 SOLANIO: Ha,—what sayest thou?—Why the end is, he hath lost
    a ship.
SALERIO: I would it might prove the end of his losses!
SOLANIO: Let me say, amen, betimes,³ lest the devil cross my
    prayer: for here he comes in the likeness of a Jew.—
20   How now, Shylock? what news among the merchants?

[Enter Shylock]

SHYLOCK: You knew, none so well, none so well as you, of my
    daughter's flight.
SALERIO: That's certain. I, for my part, knew the tailor that made
    the wings she flew withal.
25 SOLANIO: And Shylock, for his own part, knew the bird was
    fledged; and then it is the complexion of them all to leave
    the dam.⁴

¹*bit off; chewed*

²*long-windedness; speaking for a tiresome length; a lengthy lie*

³*quickly*

⁴*mother*

45

SHYLOCK: She is damn'd for it.

SALERIO: That's certain, if the devil may be her judge.

30 SHYLOCK: My own flesh and blood to rebel!

SOLANIO: Out upon it, old carrion! rebels it at these years?†

SHYLOCK: I say, my daughter is my flesh and blood.

SALERIO: There is more difference between thy flesh and hers,
than between jet[5] and ivory; more between your bloods,
35 than there is between red wine and rhenish:[6]—but tell
us, do you hear whether Antonio have had any loss at
sea or no?

SHYLOCK: There I have another bad match: a bankrupt, a
prodigal, who dare scarce show his head on the Rialto; a
40 beggar, that was used to come so smug upon the mart.[7] Let
him look to his bond: he was wont to call me usurer;—let
him look to his bond: he was wont to lend money for a
Christian courtesy;—let him look to his bond.

SALERIO: Why, I am sure, if he forfeit, thou wilt not take his
45 flesh? What's that good for?

SHYLOCK: To bait fish withal: if it will feed nothing else, it
will feed my revenge. He hath disgraced me, and hin-
dered me half a million; laughed at my losses, mocked
at my gains, scorned my nation, thwarted my bargains,
50 cooled my friends, heated mine enemies; and what's his
reason? I am a Jew: hath not a Jew eyes? hath not a Jew
hands, organs, dimensions, senses, affections, passions?
fed with the same food, hurt with the same weapons,
subject to the same diseases, healed by the same means,
55 warmed and cooled by the same winter and summer, as
a Christian is? If you prick us, do we not bleed? if you
tickle us, do we not laugh? if you poison us, do we not
die? and if you wrong us, shall we not revenge? If we are
like you in the rest, we will resemble you in that. If a Jew
60 wrong a Christian, what is his humility? revenge. If a
Christian wrong a Jew, what should his sufferance[8] be by
Christian example? why, revenge. The villany you teach
me I will execute; and it shall go hard but I will better
the instruction.

Enter a man from Antonio

65 [SERVANT:] Gentlemen, my master Antonio is at his house,
and desires to speak with you both.

[5]*black*

[6]*white (wine)*

[7]*market; fair*

[8]*patience; a will-
ingness to endure*

SALERIO: We have been up and down to seek him.

Enter Tubal

SOLANIO: Here comes another of the tribe; a third cannot be matched, unless the devil himself turn Jew.

                                      Exeunt Gentleman.

70 SHYLOCK: How now, Tubal, what news from Genoa? hast thou found my daughter?

TUBAL: I often came where I did hear of her, but cannot find her.

SHYLOCK: Why, there, there, there, there! a diamond gone, cost
75   me two thousand ducats in Frankfort! The curse never fell upon our nation till now; I never felt it till now:—two thousand ducats in that, and other precious, precious jewels.—I would my daughter were dead at my foot, and the jewels in her ear! 'would she were hearsed[9] at my foot, and the ducats
80   in her coffin! No news of them?—Why, so:—and I know not what's spent in the search. Why, thou loss upon loss! the thief gone with so much, and so much to find the thief; and no satisfaction, no revenge: nor no ill luck stirring but what lights o' my shoulders; no sighs but o' my breathing: no tears
85   but o' my shedding.

TUBAL: Yes, other men have ill luck too. Antonio, as I heard in Genoa,—

SHYLOCK: What, what, what? ill luck, ill luck?

TUBAL: Hath an argosy cast away, coming from Tripolis.

90 SHYLOCK: I thank God, I thank God:—Is it true? is it true?

TUBAL: I spoke with some of the sailors that escaped the wrack.

SHYLOCK: I thank thee, good Tubal;—Good news, good news: ha! ha!—Where? in Genoa?

95 TUBAL: Your daughter spent in Genoa, as I heard, one night, fourscore[10] ducats!

SHYLOCK: Thou stick'st a dagger in me:—I shall never see my gold again. Fourscore ducats at a sitting! fourscore ducats!

TUBAL: There came divers[11] of Antonio's creditors in my com-
100   pany to Venice, that swear he cannot choose but break.

SHYLOCK: I am very glad of it: I'll plague[12] him; I'll torture Him; I am glad of it.

TUBAL: One of them showed me a ring, that he had of your daughter for a monkey.

[9]*enclosed in a coffin*

[10]*eighty*

[11]*various, diverse, several*

[12]*to inflict with disease*

105 SHYLOCK: Out upon her! Thou torturest me, Tubal: it was
        my turquoise: I had it of Leah, when I was a bachelor: I
        would not have given it for a wilderness of monkeys.
    TUBAL: But Antonio is certainly undone.
    SHYLOCK: Nay, that's true, that's very true. Go, Tubal, fee me
110   an officer, bespeak him a fortnight before: I will have the
        heart of him, if he forfeit; forwere he out of Venice, I can
        make what merchandise I will. Go, Tubal, and meet me at
        our synagogue; go, good Tubal; at our synagogue, Tubal.
                                                    Exeunt.

[SCENE II]
[Belmont]

Enter Bassanio, Portia, Gratiano, and all their train.

PORTIA: I pray you, tarry;¹ pause a day or two,
        Before you hazard; for, in choosing wrong,
        I lose your company; therefore, forbear awhile:
        There's something tells me, (but it is not love,)
5   I would not lose you; and you know yourself,
        Hate counsels not in such a quality:²
        But lest you should not understand me well,
        (And yet a maiden hath no tongue but thought,)
        I would detain you here some month or two,
10   Before you venture for me. I could teach you
        How to choose right, but then I am forsworn;³
        So will I never be: so may you miss me;
        But if you do, you'll make me wish a sin,
        That I had been forsworn. Beshrew your eyes,†
15   They have o'erlook'd⁴ me, and divided me;
        One half of me is yours, the other half yours,—
        Mine own, I would say; but if mine, then yours,
        And so, all yours: O! these naughty times
        Put bars between the owners and their rights;
20   And so, though yours, not yours.—Prove it so,
        Let fortune go to hell for it,—not I.
        I speak too long; but 'tis to peize the time;⁵
        To eke⁶ it, and to draw it out in length,
        To stay you from election.
25 BASSANIO: Let me choose;

¹*stay*

²*"Hate does not give this counsel."*

³*"I would have broken my oath"*

⁴*put a spell on, bewitch*

⁵*"slow down the time"*

⁶*increase*

For, as I am, I live upon the rack.[†]

PORTIA: Upon the rack, Bassanio? then confess
    What treason there is mingled with your love.

BASSANIO: None, but that ugly treason of mistrust,
30   Which makes me fear the enjoying of my love:
    There may as well be amity and life
    'Tween snow and fire, as treason and my love.

PORTIA: Ay, but I fear you speak upon the rack,
    Where men enforced do speak anything.

35 BASSANIO: Promise me life, and I'll confess the truth.

PORTIA: Well, then, confess, and live.

BASSANIO: Confess, and love,
    Had been the very sum of my confession:
    O happy torment, when my torturer
40   Doth teach me answers for deliverance!
    But let me to my fortune and the caskets.

PORTIA: Away then: I am lock'd in one of them;
    If you do love me, you will find me out.
    Nerissa, and the rest, stand all aloof.
45   Let music sound, while he doth make his choice;
    Then, if he lose, he makes a swan-like end,[†]
    Fading in music: that the comparison
    May stand more proper, my eye shall be the stream,
    And watery death-bed for him. He may win;
50   And what is music then? Then music is
    Even as the flourish,[7] when true subjects bow   [7]*trumpets; fanfare*
    To a new-crowned monarch: such it is,
    As are those dulcet[8] sounds in break of day,   [8]*sweet*
    That creep into the dreaming bridegroom's ear,
55   And summon him to marriage. Now he goes,
    With no less presence, but with much more love,
    Than young Alcides,[9] when he did redeem   [9]*Hercules*
    The virgin tribute paid by howling Troy
    To the sea-monster:[†] I stand for sacrifice,
60   The rest aloof are the Dardanian[10] wives,   [10]*Trojan*
    With bleared visages, come forth to view
    The issue of the exploit. Go, Hercules!
    Live thou,[11] I live:—with much-much more dismay   [11]*"If you live"*
    I view the fight, than thou that mak'st the fray.

Here music. A song whilst Bassanio comments on the caskets to
himself.

[12]*love, affection*

[13]*Whether*

65   Tell me where is fancy[12] bred,
Or[13] in the heart, or in the head?
How begot, how nourished?

                         Reply, Reply.

It is engender'd in the eyes,
70   With gazing fed; and fancy dies
In the cradle where it lies;
Let us all ring fancy's knell;
I'll begin it,—
Ding, dong, bell.

75   **ALL:**   Ding, dong, bell.

    BASSANIO: So may the outward shows be least themselves;
The world is still deceiv'd with ornament.
In law, what plea so tainted and corrupt,
But, being season'd with a gracious voice,
80   Obscures the show of evil? In religion,
What damned error, but some sober brow
Will bless it, and approve it with a text,
Hiding the grossness with fair ornament?
There is no vice so simple, but assumes
85   Some mark of virtue on his outward parts.
How many cowards, whose hearts are all as false
As stairs of sand, wear yet upon their chins
The beards of Hercules and frowning Mars,[†]
Who, inward search'd, have livers white as milk;[†]
90   And these assume but valour's excrement[†]

[14]*feared*

To render them redoubted![14] Look on beauty,
And you shall see 'tis purchas'd by the weight;
Which therein works a miracle in nature,

[15]*makeup*

Making them lightest that wear most of it:[15]
95   So are those crisped snaky golden locks,
Which make such wanton gambols with the wind,
Upon supposed fairness, often known

[16]*wig (made from a dead person's hair)*

To be the dowry of a second head,[16]
The skull, that bred them, in the sepulchre.
100   Thus ornament is but the guiled[17] shore

[17]*misleading*

To a most dangerous sea; the beauteous scarf

[18]*unfair*

Veiling an Indian[18] beauty; in a word,
The seeming truth which cunning times put on
To entrap the wisest. Therefore, thou gaudy gold,
105   Hard food for Midas,[†] I will none of thee:

Nor none of thee, thou pale and common drudge
'Tween man and man. But thou, thou meagre lead,
Which rather threat'nest than dost promise aught,
Thy plainness moves me more than eloquence,
110   And here choose I. Joy be the consequence!
PORTIA: How all the other passions fleet to air,
As, doubtful thoughts, and rash-embrac'd despair,
And shudd'ring fear, and green-eyed jealousy.
O Love, be moderate. Allay thy ecstasy.
115   In measure rein thy joy, scant this excess;
I feel too much thy blessing, make it less,
For fear I surfeit!
    BASSANIO: What find I here?
Fair Portia's counterfeit?[19] What demi-god
120   Hath come so near creation? Move these eyes?
Or whether, riding on the balls of mine,
Seem they in motion? Here are sever'd lips,
Parted with sugar breath; so sweet a bar
Should sunder such sweet friends. Here in her hairs,
125   The painter plays the spider; and hath woven
A golden mesh to entrap the hearts of men,
Faster than gnats in cobwebs: but her eyes,—
How could he see to do them? having made one,
Methinks it should have power to steal both his,
130   And leave itself unfurnish'd. Yet look, how far,
The substance of my praise doth wrong this shadow
In underprizing[20] it, so far this shadow
Doth limp behind the substance.—Here's the scroll,
The continent and summary of my fortune.

135   *You that choose not by the view,*
    Chance as fair, and choose as true!
    Since this fortune falls to you,
    Be content, and seek no new.
    If you be well pleas'd with this,
140   *And hold your fortune for your bliss,*
    Turn you where your lady is,
    And claim her with a loving kiss.
A gentle scroll.—Fair lady, by your leave:
I come by note, to give and to receive.
145   Like one of two contending in a prize,
That thinks he hath done well in people's eyes,

[19]*picture*

[20]*minimizing*

Hearing applause and universal shout,
Giddy in spirit, still gazing in a doubt
Whether those peals of praise be his or no;
150   So, thrice fair lady, stand I, even so;
As doubtful whether what I see be true,
Until confirm'd, sign'd, ratified by you.
PORTIA: You see me, Lord Bassanio, where I stand,
Such as I am: though, for myself alone,
155   I would not be ambitious in my wish,
To wish myself much better; yet, for you,
I would be trebled twenty times myself:
A thousand times more fair, ten thousand times
More rich that only to stand high in your account,
160   I might in virtues, beauties, livings, friends,
Exceed account: but the full sum of me
Is sum of nothing; which, to term in gross,
Is, an unlesson'd girl, unschool'd, unpractis'd:
Happy in this, she is not yet so old
165   But she may learn; happier than this,
She is not bred so dull but she can learn;
Happiest of all, is, that her gentle spirit
Commits itself to yours to be directed,
As from her lord, her governor, her king.
170   Myself and what is mine, to you and yours
Is now converted: but now, I was the lord
Of this fair mansion, master of my servants,
Queen o'er myself; and even now, but now,
This house, these servants, and this same myself,
175   Are yours, my lord,—I give them with this ring;
Which when you part from, lose, or give away,
Let it presage the ruin of your love,
And be my vantage to exclaim on you.

21abandoned   BASSANIO: Madam, you have bereft21 me of all words;
180   Only my blood speaks to you in my veins,
And there is such confusion in my powers,
As, after some oration fairly spoke
By a beloved prince, there doth appear
Among the buzzing pleased multitude;
22blended   185   Where every something, being blent22 together,
23chaos   Turns to a wild23 of nothing, save of joy,
Express'd and not express'd. But when this ring
Parts from this finger, then parts life from hence;

O, then be bold to say, Bassanio's dead.

190 NERISSA: My lord and lady, it is now our time,
That have stood by, and seen our wishes prosper,
To cry, good joy; Good joy, my lord and lady!

GRATIANO: My lord Bassanio, and my gentle lady,
I wish you all the joy that you can wish;

195 For I am sure you can wish none from me:
And, when your honours mean to solemnize
The bargain of your faith, I do beseech you,
Even at that time I may be married too.

BASSANIO: With all my heart, so thou canst get a wife.

200 GRATIANO: I thank your lordship, you have got me one.
My eyes, my lord, can look as swift as yours:
You saw the mistress, I beheld the maid;
You lov'd, I lov'd for intermission.
No more pertains to me, my lord, than you.

205 Your fortune stood upon the caskets there,
And so did mine too, as the matter falls:
For wooing here, until I sweat again,
And swearing until my very roof[24] was dry
With oaths of love, at last,—if promise last,—

210 I got a promise of this fair one here,
To have her love, provided that your fortune
Achiev'd her mistress.

PORTIA: Is this true, Nerissa?

NERISSA: Madam, it is, so you stand pleas'd withal.

215 BASSANIO: And do you, Gratiano, mean good faith?

GRATIANO: Yes faith, my lord.

BASSANIO: Our feast shall be much honour'd in your marriage.

GRATIANO: We'll play[25] with them, the first boy for a thousand
ducats.

220 NERISSA: What, and stake down?[26]

GRATIANO: No; we shall ne'er win at that sport, and stake
down.
But who comes here? Lorenzo and his infidel? What, and my
old Venetian friend, Salerio?

Enter Lorenzo, Jessica, and Salerio.

BASSANIO: Lorenzo and Salerio, welcome hither;

225 If that the youth of my new interest[27] here
Have power to bid you welcome:—By your leave,

[24]*roof of my
mouth*

[25]*wager*

[26]*"make a bet?"*

[27]*position, occu-
pation*

[28]*true, real*

I bid my very[28] friends and countrymen,
Sweet Portia, welcome.
PORTIA: So do I, my lord. They are entirely welcome.
230 LORENZO: I thank your honour.—For my part, my lord,
My purpose was not to have seen you here;
But meeting with Salerio by the way,
He did entreat me, past all saying nay,
To come with him along.
235 SALERIO: I did, my lord,
And I have reason for it. Signior Antonio
Commends him to you.
BASSANIO: Ere I ope his letter,
I pray you tell me how my good friend doth.
240 SALERIO: Not sick, my lord, unless it be in mind;
Nor well, unless in mind: his letter there
Will show you his estate.   *Opens the letter.*
GRATIANO: Nerissa, cheer yon stranger; bid her welcome.
Your hand, Salerio. What's the news from Venice?
245   How doth that royal merchant, good Antonio?
I know he will be glad of our success;
We are the Jasons, we have won the fleece.[†]
SALERIO: I would you had won the fleece that he hath lost!
PORTIA: There are some shrewd contents in yon same paper,
250   That steals the colour from Bassanio's cheek;
Some dear friend dead; else nothing in the world
Could turn so much the constitution
Of any constant man. What, worse and worse?—
With leave, Bassanio; I am half yourself,
255   And I must freely have the half of anything
That this same paper brings you.
BASSANIO: O sweet Portia,
Here are a few of the unpleasant'st words
That ever blotted paper! Gentle lady,
260   When I did first impart my love to you,
I freely told you, all the wealth I had
Ran in my veins,—I was a gentleman;
And then I told you true: and yet, dear lady,
Rating myself at nothing, you shall see,
265   How much I was a braggart. When I told you
My state was nothing, I should then have told you
That I was worse than nothing; for, indeed,
I have engag'd myself to a dear friend,

       Engag'd my friend to his mere enemy,
270   To feed my means. Here is a letter, lady;
       The paper as the body of my friend,
       And every word in it a gaping wound,
       Issuing life-blood. But is it true, Salerio?
       Have all his ventures fail'd? What, not one hit?
275   From Tripolis, from Mexico, and England,
       From Lisbon, Barbary, and India?
       And not one vessel 'scape the dreadful touch
       Of merchant-marring rocks?
  SALERIO: Not one, my lord.
280   Besides, it should appear, that if he had
       The present money to discharge the Jew,
       He would not take it. Never did I know
       A creature that did bear the shape of man,
       So keen and greedy to confound a man:
285   He plies the duke at morning, and at night,
       And doth impeach the freedom of the state
       If they deny him justice: twenty merchants,
       The duke himself, and the magnificoes
       Of greatest port, have all persuaded with him;
290   But none can drive him from the envious plea
       Of forfeiture, of justice, and his bond.
  JESSICA: When I was with him, I have heard him swear
       To Tubal, and to Chus, his countrymen,
       That he would rather have Antonio's flesh,
295   Than twenty times the value of the sum
       That he did owe him; and I know, my lord,
       If law, authority, and power deny not,
       It will go hard with poor Antonio.
  PORTIA: Is it your dear friend that is thus in trouble?
300 BASSANIO: The dearest friend to me, the kindest man,
       The best-condition'd and unwearied spirit
       In doing courtesies; and one in whom
       The ancient Roman honour more appears,
       Than any that draws breath in Italy.
305 PORTIA: What sum owes he the Jew?
  BASSANIO: For me, three thousand ducats.
  PORTIA: What, no more?
       Pay him six thousand, and deface the bond;
       Double six thousand, and then treble that,
310   Before a friend of this description

Shall lose a hair through Bassanio's fault.
First go with me to church, and call me wife,
And then away to Venice to your friend;
For never shall you lie by Portia's side
315   With an unquiet soul. You shall have gold
To pay the petty debt twenty times over;
When it is paid, bring your true friend along:
My maid Nerissa and myself, meantime,
Will live as maids and widows. Come, away,
320   For you shall hence upon your wedding-day:
Bid your friends welcome, show a merry cheer:
Since you are dear bought, I will love you dear.
But let me hear the letter of your friend.
BASSANIO: [Reads] *Sweet Bassanio, my ships have all miscar-*
325   *ried, my creditors grow cruel, my estate is very low, my bond*
to the Jew is forfeit; and since, in paying it, it is impossible I
should live, all debts are cleared between you and I, if I might
but see you at my death; Notwithstanding, use your pleasure:
if your love do not persuade you to come, let not my letter.
330 PORTIA: O love, despatch all business, and be gone.
BASSANIO: Since I have your good leave to go away,
I will make haste: but, till I come again,
No bed shall e'er be guilty of my stay,
335   Nor rest be interposer 'twixt us twain.

Exeunt.

[SCENE III]
[Venice]

Enter the Jew, and Solanio, and Antonio, and the Jailor.

SHYLOCK: Gaoler, look to him. tell not me of mercy;—
This is the fool that lent out money gratis;—
Gaoler, look to him.
ANTONIO: Hear me yet, good Shylock.
5 SHYLOCK: I'll have my bond; speak not against my bond;
I have sworn an oath that I will have my bond;
Thou call'dst me dog, before thou hadst a cause;
But, since I am a dog, beware my fangs:

The duke shall grant me justice.—I do wonder,
10   Thou naughty[1] gaoler, that thou art so fond
   To come abroad with him at his request.

ANTONIO: I pray thee, hear me speak.

SHYLOCK: I'll have my bond; I will not hear thee speak;
   I'll have my bond; and therefore speak no more.
15   I'll not be made a soft and dull-ey'd[2] fool,
   To shake the head, relent, and sigh, and yield
   To Christian intercessors. Follow not;
   I'll have no speaking; I will have my bond.   *Exit Jew.*

SOLANIO: It is the most impenetrable cur[3]
20   That ever kept with men.

ANTONIO: Let him alone;
   I'll follow him no more with bootless[4] prayers.
   He seeks my life; his reason well I know.
   I oft deliver'd from his forfeitures,
25   Many that have at times made moan to me;
   Therefore he hates me.

SOLANIO: I am sure, the Duke
   Will never grant this forfeiture to hold.

ANTONIO: The Duke cannot deny the course of law,
30   For the commodity[5] that strangers have
   With us in Venice; if it be denied,
   'Twill much impeach[6] the justice of the state;
   Since that the trade and profit of the city
   Consisteth of all nations. Therefore, go
35   These griefs and losses have so 'bated[7] me,
   That I shall hardly spare a pound of flesh
   To-morrow, to my bloody creditor.
   Well, gaoler, on:—Pray God, Bassanio come
   To see me pay his debt, and then I care not!
                                        Exeunt.

[SCENE IV]
[Belmont]

Enter Portia, Nerissa, Lorenzo, Jessica, and a man of Portia [Balthasar].

LORENZO: Madam, although I speak it in your presence,
   You have a noble and a true conceit[1]

---

[1]*wicked*

[2]*naïve, gullible*

[3]*dog; coward*

[4]*fruitless*

[5]*convenience of doing business*

[6]*call into question*

[7]*weakened*

[1]*image*

Of god-like amity; which appears most strongly
In bearing thus the absence of your lord.
5   But, if you knew to whom you show this honour,
How true a gentleman you send relief,
How dear a lover of my lord your husband,
I know you would be prouder of the work,
Than customary bounty can enforce you.
10 PORTIA: I never did repent for doing good,
Nor shall not now; for in companions
That do converse and waste the time together,
Whose souls do bear an equal yoke of love,
There must be needs a like proportion
15   Of lineaments, of manners, and of spirit;
Which makes me think, that this Antonio,
Being the bosom lover of my lord,
Must needs be like my lord. If it be so,
How little is the cost I have bestow'd,
20   In purchasing the semblance of my soul
From out the state of hellish cruelty!
This comes too near the praising of myself,
Therefore, no more of it: hear other things.
Lorenzo, I commit into your hands
25   The husbandry and manage of my house,
Until my lord's return; for mine own part,
I have toward heaven breathed a secr't vow,
To live in prayer and contemplation,
Only attended by Nerissa here,
30   Until her husband and my lord's return:
There is a monastery two miles off,
And there will we abide. I do desire you
Not to deny this imposition,
The which my love, and some necessity,
35   Now lays upon you.
LORENZO: Madam, with all my heart,
I shall obey you in all fair commands.
PORTIA: My people do already know my mind,
And will acknowledge you and Jessica,
40   In place of Lord Bassanio and myself.
So fare you well, till we shall meet again.
LORENZO: Fair thoughts and happy hours attend on you!
JESSICA: I wish your ladyship all heart's content.
PORTIA: I thank you for your wish, and am well pleas'd

45 To wish it back on you: fare you well, Jessica.
                              Exeunt [Jessica and Lorenzo]
    Now, Balthasar,
    As I have ever found thee honest, true,
    So let me find thee still: Take this same letter,
    And use thou all the endeavour of a man
50 In speed to Padua; see thou render this
    Into my cousin's hand, Doctor Bellario;
    And, look, what notes and garments he doth give thee,
    Bring them, I pray thee, with imagin'd speed
    Unto the Tranect,[2] to the common ferry   ²*a ferry*
55 Which trades to Venice:—Waste no time in words,
    But get thee gone; I shall be there before thee.
BALTHASAR: Madam, I go with all convenient speed.
PORTIA: Come on, Nerissa; I have work in hand,
    That you yet know not of; we'll see our husbands
60 Before they think of us.
NERISSA: Shall they see us?
PORTIA: They shall, Nerissa; but in such a habit,[3]   ³*"in such attire"*
    That they shall think we are accomplished[4]   ⁴*"we are men"*
    With that we lack. I'll hold thee any wager,
65 When we are both accoutred like young men,
    I'll prove the prettier fellow of the two,
    And wear my dagger with the braver grace;
    And speak, between the change of man and boy,
    With a reed voice;† and turn two mincing steps
70 Into a manly stride; and speak of frays,
    Like a fine bragging youth: and tell quaint lies,
    How honourable ladies sought my love,
    Which I denying, they fell sick and died;
    I could not do withal; then I'll repent,
75 And wish, for all that, that I had not kill'd them:
    And twenty of these puny lies I'll tell,
    That men shall swear I have discontinued school
    Above a twelvemonth:[5]—I have within my mind   ⁵*"only one year out of school"*
    A thousand raw tricks of these bragging Jacks,
80 Which I will practise.
NERISSA: Why, shall we turn to men?†
PORTIA: Fie! what a question's that,
    If thou wert near a lewd interpreter!
    But come, I'll tell thee all my whole device

85   When I am in my coach, which stays for us
        At the park gate; and therefore haste away,
        For we must measure twenty miles to-day.

                                                        Exeunt.

                            [SCENE V]
                            [The same]

        Enter Clown [Launcelot] and Jessica.

        LAUNCELOT: Yes, truly;—for, look you, the sins of the father
            are to be laid upon the children; therefore, I promise you
            I fear you. I was always plain¹ with you, and so now I
            speak my agitation of the matter: therefore, be of good
5   chee; for, truly, I think you are damned. There is but one
            hope in it that can do you any good; and that is but a kind
            of bastard hope neither.
        JESSICA: And what hope is that, I pray thee?
        LAUNCELOT: Marry, you may partly hope that your father got
10   you not, that you are not the Jew's daughter.
        JESSICA: That were a kind of bastard hope, indeed; so, the sins
            of my mother should be visited upon me.
        LAUNCELOT: Truly then I fear you are damned both by father
            and mother: thus when I shun Scylla, your father, I fall
15   into Charybdis,† your mother: well, you are gone both
            ways.
        JESSICA: I shall be saved by my husband; he hath made me a
            Christian.
        LAUNCELOT: Truly, the more to blame he: we were Christians
20   enow² before; e'en as many as could well live, one by
            another: This making Christians will raise the price of
            hogs; if we grow all to be pork-eaters† we shall not shortly
            have a rasher³ on the coals for money.

        [Enter Lorenzo.]

        JESSICA: I'll tell my husband, Launcelot, what you say; here
25   he comes.
        LORENZO: I shall grow jealous of you shortly, Launcelot, if you
            thus get my wife into corners.
        JESSICA: Nay, you need not fear us, Lorenzo. Launcelot and I

¹*honest, straight-forward*

²*enough*

³*a piece of bacon*

30 are out: He tells me flatly, there is no mercy for me in heaven, because I am a Jew's daughter: and he says, you are no good member of the commonwealth; for in converting Jews to Christians, you raise the price of pork.

LORENZO: I shall answer that better to the commonwealth, than you can the getting up of the negro's belly; the Moor is with

35 child by you, Launcelot.

LAUNCELOT: It is much, that the Moor should be more than reason:[4] but if she be less than an honest[5] woman, she is, indeed more than I took her for.

LORENZO: How every fool can play upon the word! I think the

40 best grace of wit will shortly turn into silence; and discourse grow commendable in none only but parrots.—Go in, sirrah; bid them prepare for dinner.

LAUNCELOT: That is done, sir, they have all stomachs.

LORENZO: Goodly Lord, what a wit-snapper are you! then bid

45 them prepare dinner.

LAUNCELOT: That is done too, sir: only, cover is the word.

LORENZO: Will you cover, then, sir?

LAUNCELOT: Not so, sir, neither; I know my duty.

LORENZO: Yet more quarrelling with occasion! Wilt thou show

50 the whole wealth of thy wit in an instant? I pray thee, understand a plain man in his plain meaning; go to thy fellows; bid them cover the table,[6] serve in the meat, and we will come in to dinner.

LAUNCELOT: For the table, sir, it shall be served in; for the meat,

55 sir, it shall be covered; for your coming into dinner, sir, why, let it be as humours and conceits shall govern. *Exit Clown.*

LORENZO: O dear discretion, how his words are suited!
The fool hath planted in his memory
An army of good words; and I do know

60 A many fools, that stand in better place,
Garnish'd like him, that for a tricksy word
Defy the matter. How cheer'st thou, Jessica?
And now, good sweet, say thy opinion;—
How dost thou like the Lord Bassanio's wife?

65 JESSICA: Past all expressing. It is very meet,
The Lord Bassanio live an upright life;
For, having such a blessing in his lady,
He finds the joys of heaven here on earth;
And, if on earth he do not mean it, then

70 In reason he should never come to heaven.

[4]*larger than she should reasonably (if she were not pregnant)*

[5]*chaste, pure, virginal*

[6]*set the table*

Why, if two gods should play some heavenly match,
And on the wager lay two earthly women,
And Portia one, there must be something else
Pawn'd with the other; for the poor rude world
75   Hath not her fellow.
LORENZO: Even such a husband
Hast thou of me, as she is for a wife.
JESSICA: Nay, but ask my opinion too of that.
LORENZO: I will anon; first, let us go to dinner.
80 JESSICA: Nay, let me praise you, while I have a stomach.
LORENZO: No, pray thee, let it serve for table-talk;
Then, howso'er thou speak'st, 'mong other things
I shall digest it.
JESSICA: Well, I'll set you forth.

                                                      Exeunt.

ACT IV

[SCENE I]
[Venice]

Enter the Duke, the Magnificoes, Antonio, Bassanio, and Gratiano,
[Salerio, and others]

DUKE: What, is Antonio here?
ANTONIO: Ready, so please your grace.
DUKE: I am sorry for thee; thou art come to answer
     A stony adversary, an inhuman wretch
5   Uncapable of pity, void and empty
     From any dram¹ of mercy.   ¹*trace, ounce*
ANTONIO: I have heard
     Your grace hath ta'en great pains to qualify
     His rigorous course; but since he stands obdurate,
10   And that no lawful means can carry me
     Out of his envy's reach, I do oppose
     My patience to his fury; and am arm'd
     To suffer, with a quietness of spirit,
     The very tyranny and rage of his.
15 DUKE: Go one, and call the Jew into the court.
SALERIO: He is ready at the door: he comes, my lord.

Enter Shylock

DUKE: Make room, and let him stand before our face.
     Shylock, the world thinks, and I think so too,
     That thou but lead'st this fashion of thy malice
20   To the last hour of act; and then, 'tis thought
     Thou'lt show thy mercy and remorse, more strange
     Than is thy strange apparent cruelty:
     And where thou now exact'st the penalty,
     (Which is a pound of this poor merchant's flesh,)
25   Thou wilt not only loose the forfeiture,

2*part, portion*

But, touch'd with human gentleness and love,
Forgive a moiety[2] of the principal;
Glancing an eye of pity on his losses,
That have of late so huddled on his back,
30   Enough to press a royal merchant down,
And pluck commiseration of his state

3*unfeeling, hard*

From brassy[3] bosoms, and rough hearts of flint,
From stubborn Turks and Tartars, never train'd
To offices of tender courtesy.
35   We all expect a gentle answer, Jew.
SHYLOCK: I have possess'd your grace of what I purpose;
And by our holy Sabbath have I sworn,
To have the due and forfeit of my bond:
If you deny it, let the danger light
40   Upon your charter, and your city's freedom.
You'll ask me, why I rather choose to have
A weight of carrion flesh, than to receive
Three thousand ducats: I'll not answer that:
But, say, it is my humour. is it answer'd?
45   What, if my house be troubled with a rat
And I be pleas'd to give ten thousand ducats

4*poisoned*

To have it ban'd[4]? What, are you answer'd yet?
Some men there are love not a gaping pig;
Some, that are mad if they behold a cat;
50   And others, when the bagpipe sings i' the nose,
Cannot contain their urine: for affection,
Master of passion, sways it to the mood

5*"impulse deter-mines the mind's likes and dis-likes"*

Of what it likes, or loathes.[5] Now, for your answer.
As there is no firm reason to be render'd,
55   Why he, cannot abide a gaping pig;
Why he, a harmless necessary cat;
Why he, a woollen bagpipe,—but of force
Must yield to such inevitable shame,
As to offend himself, being offended;
60   So can I give no reason, nor I will not,

6*settled*

More than a lodged[6] hate, and a certain loathing,
I bear Antonio, that I follow thus
A losing suit against him. Are you answer'd?
BASSANIO: This is no answer, thou unfeeling man,

7*constant flow*

65   To excuse the current[7] of thy cruelty.
SHYLOCK: I am not bound to please thee with my answers.
BASSANIO: Do all men kill the things they do not love?

SHYLOCK: Hates any man the thing he would not kill?
BASSANIO: Every offence is not a hate at first.
70 SHYLOCK: What, wouldst thou have a serpent sting thee twice?
ANTONIO: I pray you, think you question with the Jew,
      You may as well go stand upon the beach,
      And bid the main flood bate his[8] usual height;
      You may as well use question with the wolf,
75   Why he hath made the ewe bleat for the lamb;
      You may as well forbid the mountain pines
      To wag their high tops, and to make no noise
      When they are fretten with the gusts of heaven;
      You may as well do anything most hard,
80   As seek to soften that (than which what's harder?)
      His Jewish heart.—therefore, I do beseech you,
      Make no more offers, use no farther means,
      But, with all brief and plain conveniency,
      Let me have judgment and the Jew his will.
85 BASSANIO: For thy three thousand ducats here is six.
SHYLOCK: If every ducat in six thousand ducats
      Were in six parts, and every part a ducat,
      I would not draw them,—I would have my bond.
DUKE: How shalt thou hope for mercy, rendering none?
90 SHYLOCK: What judgment shall I dread, doing no wrong?
      You have among you many a purchas'd slave,
      Which, like your asses, and your dogs, and mules,
      You use in abject and in slavish parts,
      Because you bought them.—shall I say to you
95   Let them be free, marry them to your heirs?
      Why sweat they under burthens?[9] let their beds
      Be made as soft as yours, and let their palates[10]
      Be season'd with such viands?[11] You will answer,
      The slaves are ours:—so do I answer you.
100   The pound of flesh, which I demand of him,
      Is dearly bought; 'tis mine, and I will have it:
      If you deny me, fie upon your law!
      There is no force in the decrees of Venice:
      I stand for judgment: answer, shall I have it?
105 DUKE: Upon my power, I may dismiss this court,
      Unless Bellario, a learned doctor,
      Whom I have sent for to determine this,
      Come here to-day.
SALERIO: My lord, here stays without,

[8]*reduce its*

[9]*burdens*

[10]*mouths*

[11]*food*

110   A messenger with letters from the doctor,
       New come from Padua.
    DUKE: Bring us the letters. Call the messenger.
    BASSANIO: Good cheer, Antonio! What, man! courage yet!
       The Jew shall have my flesh, blood, bones, and all,
115   Ere thou shalt lose for me one drop of blood.
    ANTONIO: I am a tainted wether[12] of the flock,
       Meetest[13] for death; the weakest kind of fruit
       Drops earliest to the ground, and so let me:
       You cannot better be employ'd, Bassanio,
120   Than to live still, and write mine epitaph.

    Enter Nerissa [disguised].

    DUKE: Came you, from Padua, from Bellario?
    NERISSA: From both, my lord: Bellario greets your grace.
    BASSANIO: Why dost thou whet[14] thy knife so earnestly?
    SHYLOCK: To cut the forfeiture from that bankrupt there.
    GRATIANO: Not on thy sole, but on thy soul, harsh Jew,
125   Thou mak'st thy knife keen; but no metal can,
       No, not the hangman's axe, bear half the keenness
       Of thy sharp envy. Can no prayers pierce thee?
    SHYLOCK: No, none that thou hast wit enough to make.
    GRATIANO: O, be thou damn'd, inexecrable dog!
130   And for thy life let justice be accus'd.
       Thou almost mak'st me waver in my faith,
       To hold opinion with Pythagoras,†
       That souls of animals infuse themselves
       Into the trunks of men: thy currish spirit
135   Govern'd a wolf, who, hang'd for human slaughter,
       Even from the gallows did his fell[15] soul fleet,[16]
       And, whilst thou lay'st in thy unhallow'd dam,[17]
       Infus'd itself in thee; for thy desires
       Are wolvish, bloody, sterved, and ravenous.
140 SHYLOCK: Till thou canst rail the seal from off my bond,
       Thou but offend'st thy lungs to speak so loud:
       Repair thy wit, good youth; or it will fall
       To cureless ruin.—I stand here for law.
    DUKE: This letter from Bellario doth commend
145   A young and learned doctor to our court:—
       Where is he?

[12]*sheep*

[13]*Most suitable*

[14]*sharpen*

[15]*cruel*

[16]*flee*

[17]*"your unholy mother*

NERISSA: He attendeth here hard by,
    To know your answer, whether you'll admit him.
150 DUKE: With all my heart:—Some three or four of you
    Go give him courteous conduct to this place.—
    Meantime, the court shall hear Bellario's letter.
CLERK: *Your grace shall understand, that at the receipt of your letter,*
    I am very sick: but in the instant that your messenger came, in
155   *loving visitation was with me a young doctor of Rome; his name*
    is Balthasar: I acquainted him with the cause in controversy
    between the Jew and Antonio the merchant: we turned o'er many
    books together: he is furnished with my opinion; which, bettered
    with his own learning (the greatness whereof I cannot enough
160   *commend), comes with him, at my importunity, to fill up your*
    grace's request in my stead. I beseech you, let his lack of years
    be no impediment to let him lack a reverend estimation; for I
    never knew so young a body with so old a head. I leave him to
    your gracious acceptance, whose trial shall better publish his
165   *commendation.*

Enter Portia, [disguised] Balthasar

DUKE: You hear the learn'd Bellario, what he writes:
    And here, I take it, is the doctor come.—
    Give me your hand. Come you from old Bellario?
PORTIA: I did, my lord.
170 DUKE: You are welcome: take your place.
    Are you acquainted with the difference
    That holds this present question in the court?
PORTIA: I am informed thoroughly of the cause.
    Which is the merchant here, and which the Jew?
175 DUKE: Antonio and old Shylock, both stand forth.
PORTIA: Is your name Shylock?
SHYLOCK: Shylock is my name.
PORTIA: Of a strange nature is the suit you follow;
    Yet in such rule, that the Venetian law
180   Cannot impugn[18] you as you do proceed.—
    You stand within his danger, do you not?
ANTONIO: Ay, so he says.
PORTIA: Do you confess the bond?
ANTONIO: I do.
185 PORTIA: Then must the Jew be merciful.
SHYLOCK: On what compulsion[19] must I? tell me that.

[18]*find fault with*

[19]*irresistible*
impulse

PORTIA: The quality of mercy is not strain'd,
It droppeth, as the gentle rain from heaven
Upon the place beneath: it is twice bless'd;
190   It blesseth him that gives, and him that takes:
'Tis mightiest in the mightiest; it becomes
The throned monarch better than his crown;
His sceptre shows the force of temporal power,
The attribute to awe and majesty,
195   Wherein doth sit the dread and fear of kings;
But mercy is above this sceptred sway,
It is enthroned in the hearts of kings,
It is an attribute to God himself;
And earthly power doth then show likest God's
200   When mercy seasons justice. Therefore, Jew,
Though justice be thy plea, consider this—
That in the course of justice, none of us
Should see salvation: we do pray for mercy;
And that same prayer, doth teach us all to render
205   The deeds of mercy. I have spoke thus much,
To mitigate the justice of thy plea,
Which if thou follow, this strict court of Venice
Must needs give sentence 'gainst the merchant there.
SHYLOCK: My deeds upon my head! I crave the law,
210   The penalty and forfeit of my bond.
PORTIA: Is he not able to discharge the money?
BASSANIO: Yes, here I tender it for him in the court;
Yea, twice the sum: if that will not suffice,
I will be bound to pay it ten times o'er,
215   On forfeit of my hands, my head, my heart:
If this will not suffice, it must appear
That malice bears down truth. And I beseech you,
Wrest once the law to your authority:
To do a great right, do a little wrong;
220   And curb this cruel devil of his will.
PORTIA: It must not be; there is no power in Venice
Can alter a decree established:
'Twill be recorded for a precedent,
And many an error, by the same example
225   Will rush into the state: it cannot be.
SHYLOCK: A Daniel† come to judgment! yea, a Daniel!
O wise young judge, how I do honour thee!
PORTIA: I pray you, let me look upon the bond.

SHYLOCK: Here, 'tis, most reverend doctor, here it is.
230 PORTIA: Shylock, there's thrice thy money offer'd thee.
SHYLOCK: An oath, an oath, I have an oath in heaven:
    Shall I lay perjury upon my soul?
    No, not for Venice.
PORTIA: Why, this bond is forfeit;
235   And lawfully by this the Jew may claim
    A pound of flesh, to be by him cut off
    Nearest the merchant's heart.—Be merciful;
    Take thrice thy money; bid me tear the bond.
SHYLOCK: When it is paid according to the tenor.
240   It doth appear you are a worthy judge;
    You know the law, your exposition
    Hath been most sound; I charge you by the law,
    Whereof you are a well-deserving pillar,
    Proceed to judgment: by my soul I swear
245   There is no power in the tongue of man
    To alter me: I stay here on my bond.
ANTONIO: Most heartily I do beseech the court
    To give the judgment.
PORTIA: Why then, thus it is:
250   You must prepare your bosom for his knife.
SHYLOCK: O noble judge! O excellent young man!
PORTIA: For the intent and purpose of the law,
    Hath full relation to the penalty,
    Which here appeareth due upon the bond;—
255 SHYLOCK: 'Tis very true: O wise and upright judge!
    How much more elder art thou than thy looks!
PORTIA: Therefore lay bare your bosom.
SHYLOCK: Ay, his breast:
    So says the bond;—doth it not, noble judge?
260   Nearest his heart, those are the very words.
PORTIA: It is so. Are there balance here to weigh
    The flesh?
SHYLOCK: I have them ready.
PORTIA: Have by some surgeon, Shylock, on your charge,
265   To stop his wounds, lest he do bleed to death.
SHYLOCK: Is it so nominated in the bond?
PORTIA: It is not so express'd, but what of that?
    'Twere good you do so much for charity.
SHYLOCK: I cannot find it; 'tis not in the bond.
270 PORTIA: Come, merchant, have you any thing to say?

ANTONIO: But little; I am arm'd, and well prepar'd.—
Give me your hand, Bassannio: fare you well!
Grieve not that I am fallen to this for you;
For herein Fortune shows herself more kind
275   Than is her custom: it is still her use,
To let the wretched man out-live his wealth,
To view with hollow eye, and wrinkled brow,
An age of poverty; from which lingering penance
Of such misery doth she cut me off.
280   Commend me to your honourable wife:
Tell her the process of Antonio's end,

Antonio & Bassino ←———— Say, how I lov'd you, speak me fair in death;

And, when the tale is told, bid her be judge
Whether Bassanio had not once a love.
285   Repent not you that you shall lose your friend,
And he repents not that he pays your debt;
For, if the Jew do cut but deep enough,
I'll pay it instantly with all my heart.
BASSANIO: Antonio, I am married to a wife,
290   Which is as dear to me as life itself;
But life itself, my wife, and all the world
Are not with me esteem'd above thy life;
I would lose all, ay, sacrifice them all
Here to this devil, to deliver you.
295 PORTIA: Your wife would give you little thanks for that,
If she were by, to hear you make the offer.
GRATIANO: I have a wife, whom I protest I love;
I would she were in heaven, so she could
Entreat some power to change this currish Jew.
300 NERISSA: 'Tis well you offer it behind her back;
The wish would make else an unquiet house.
SHYLOCK: These be the Christian husbands: I have a
     daughter;
Would any of the stock of Barrabas
305   Had been her husband rather, than a Christian!
We trifle time; I pray thee pursue sentence.
PORTIA: A pound of that same merchant's flesh is thine;
The court awards it, and the law doth give it.
SHYLOCK: Most rightful judge!
310 PORTIA: And you must cut this flesh from off his breast;
The law allows it, and the court awards it.
SHYLOCK: Most learned judge!—A sentence! come, prepare!

PORTIA: Tarry a little;—there is something else.—
　　This bond doth give thee here no jot of blood;
315　The words expressly are, a pound of flesh:
　　Take then thy bond, take thou thy pound of flesh;
　　But, in the cutting it, if thou dost shed
　　One drop of Christian blood, thy lands and goods
　　Are, by the laws of Venice, confiscate
320　Unto the state of Venice.
GRATIANO:　　　　　　O upright judge!—Mark, Jew;—O
　　learned judge!
SHYLOCK: Is that the law?
PORTIA: Thyself shalt see the act:
325　For, as thou urgest justice, be assur'd
　　Thou shalt have justice, more than thou desirest.
GRATIANO: O learned judge!—Mark, Jew;—a learned judge!
SHYLOCK: I take this offer then,—pay the bond thrice
　　And let the Christian go.
330 BASSANIO:　　　　　　Here is the money.
PORTIA: Soft;—
　　The Jew shall have all justice;—soft;—no haste;—
　　He shall have nothing but the penalty.
GRATIANO: O Jew! an upright judge, a learned judge!
335 PORTIA: Therefore prepare thee to cut off the flesh.
　　Shed thou no blood; nor cut thou less, nor more,
　　But just a pound of flesh: if thou tak'st more,
　　Or less, than a just pound,—be it but so much
　　As makes it light, or heavy, in the substance,
340　Or the division of the twentieth part
　　Of one poor scruple,—nay, if the scale do turn
　　But in the estimation of a hair,—
　　Thou diest and all thy goods are confiscate.
GRATIANO: A second Daniel, a Daniel, Jew!
345　Now, infidel, I have thee on the hip.
PORTIA: Why doth the Jew pause? take thy forfeiture.
SHYLOCK: Give me my principal, and let me go.
BASSANIO: I have it ready for thee; here it is.
PORTIA: He hath refus'd it in the open court;
350　He shall have merely justice and his bond.
GRATIANO: A Daniel, still say I; a second Daniel!—
　　I thank thee, Jew, for teaching me that word.
SHYLOCK: Shall I not have barely my principal?
PORTIA: Thou shalt have nothing but the forfeiture,

355   To be so taken at thy peril, Jew.
       SHYLOCK: Why, then the devil give him good of it!
       I'll stay no longer question.
       PORTIA: Tarry, Jew;
       The law hath yet another hold on you.
360   It is enacted in the laws of Venice,—
       If it be proved against an alien
       That by direct or indirect attempts
       He seek the life of any citizen,
       The party 'gainst the which he doth contrive,
365   Shall seize one half his goods; the other half
       Comes to the privy coffer of the state;
       And the offender's life lies in the mercy
       Of the duke only, 'gainst all other voice.
       In which predicament, I say, thou stand'st:
370   For it appears by manifest proceeding,
       That, indirectly, and directly too,
       Thou hast contriv'd against the very life
       Of the defendant; and thou hast incurr'd
       The danger formerly by me rehears'd.
375   Down, therefore, and beg mercy of the duke.
       GRATIANO: Beg that thou mayst have leave to hang thyself:
       And yet, thy wealth being forfeit to the state,
       Thou hast not left the value of a cord;
       Therefore thou must be hang'd at the state's charge.
380 DUKE: That thou shalt see the difference of our spirits,
       I pardon thee thy life before thou ask it:
       For half thy wealth, it is Antonio's;
       The other half comes to the general state,
       Which humbleness may drive unto a fine.[20]
385 PORTIA: Ay, for the state; not for Antonio.
       SHYLOCK: Nay, take my life and all; pardon not that:
       You take my house when you do take the prop
       That doth sustain my house; you take my life,
       When you do take the means whereby I live.
390 PORTIA: What mercy can you render him, Antonio?
       GRATIANO: A halter gratis; nothing else, for God's sake!
       ANTONIO: So please my lord the duke, and all the court
       To quit the fine for one half of his goods;
       I am content, so he will let me have
395   The other half in use, to render it,
       Upon his death, unto the gentleman

[20]*"reduce to a fine"*

That lately stole his daughter;
Two things provided more,—that for this favour,
He presently become a Christian;
400   The other, that he do record a gift,
Here in the court, of all he dies possess'd,
Unto his son Lorenzo and his daughter.
DUKE: He shall do this; or else I do recant
The pardon that I late pronounced here.
405 PORTIA: Art thou contented, Jew? what dost thou say?
SHYLOCK: I am content.
PORTIA: Clerk, draw a deed of gift.
SHYLOCK: I pray you give me leave to go from hence:
I am not well; send the deed after me,
410   And I will sign it.
DUKE: Get thee gone, but do it.
GRATIANO: In christening, shalt thou have two god-fathers;
Had I been judge, thou shouldst have had ten more,
To bring thee to the gallows, not the font.   *Exit [Shylock]*
415 DUKE: Sir, I entreat you home with me to dinner.
PORTIA: I humbly do desire your grace of pardon.
I must away this night toward Padua,
And it is meet I presently set forth.
DUKE: I am sorry that your leisure serves you not.
420   Antonio, gratify this gentleman,
For, in my mind, you are much bound to him.
                              Exit Duke *and his train.*
BASSANIO: Most worthy gentleman, I, and my friend,
Have by your wisdom been this day acquitted
Of grievous penalties; in lieu whereof,
425   Three thousand ducats, due unto the Jew,
We freely cope your courteous pains withal.
ANTONIO: And stand indebted, over and above,
In love and service to you evermore.
PORTIA: He is well paid that is well satisfied:
430   And I, delivering you, am satisfied,
And therein do account myself well paid;
My mind was never yet more mercenary.
I pray you, know me, when we meet again;
I wish you well, and so I take my leave.
435 BASSANIO: Dear sir, of force I must attempt you further;
Take some remembrance of us, as a tribute,
Not as fee: grant me two things, I pray you,

Not to deny me, and to pardon me.

PORTIA: You press me far, and therefore I will yield.

440   [*To* Antonio] Give me your gloves, I'll wear them for
                 your sake;

              [*To* Bassanio] And, for your love, I'll take this ring from
                 you:—

              Do not draw back your hand; I'll take no more;

445   And you in love shall not deny me this.

BASSANIO: This ring, good sir?—alas, it is a trifle:
              I will not shame myself to give you this.

PORTIA: I will have nothing else but only this;
              And now, methinks, I have a mind to it.

450 BASSANIO: There's more depends on this than on the value.
              The dearest ring in Venice will I give you,
              And find it out by proclamation;
              Only for this I pray you pardon me.

PORTIA: I see, sir, you are liberal in offers:

455   You taught me first to beg; and now, methinks,
              You teach me how a beggar should be answer'd.

BASSANIO: Good sir, this ring was given me by my wife;
              And, when she put it on, she made me vow
              That I should neither sell, nor give, nor lose it.

460 PORTIA: That 'scuse serves many men to save their gifts.
              An if your wife be not a mad woman,
              And know how well I have deserv'd the ring,
              She would not hold out enemy for ever,
              For giving it to me. Well, peace be with you!

                                    Exeunt [Portia and Nerissa]

465 ANTONIO: My Lord Bassanio, let him have the ring,
              Let his deservings, and my love withal,
              Be valued 'gainst your wife's commandment.

BASSANIO: Go, Gratiano, run and overtake him;
              Give him the ring; and bring him, if thou canst,

470   Unto Antonio's house:—away! make haste.

                                    Exit Gratiano.

              Come, you and I will thither presently;
              And in the morning early will we both
              Fly toward Belmont: come, Antonio.

                                    Exeunt.

[SCENE II]
[The same]

Enter Portia and Nerissa.

PORTIA: Inquire the Jew's house out, give him this deed,
   And let him sign it; we'll away to-night,
   And be a day before our husbands home.
   This deed will be well welcome to Lorenzo.

Enter Gratiano

5 GRATIANO: Fair sir, you are well o'erta'en:
   My Lord Bassanio, upon more advice,
   Hath sent you here this ring, and doth entreat
   Your company at dinner.
PORTIA: That cannot be:
10   His ring I do accept most thankfully,
   And so, I pray you, tell him: furthermore,
   I pray you, show my youth old Shylock's house.
GRATIANO: That will I do.
NERISSA: Sir, I would speak with you:—
15   I'll see if I can get my husband's ring,
   Which I did make him swear to keep for ever.
PORTIA: Thou may'st, I warrant we shall have old¹ swearing,   ¹*a lot of*
   That they did give the rings away to men;
   But we'll outface² them, and outswear them too.   ²*boldly contradict*
20   Away! make haste; thou know'st where I will tarry.
NERISSA: Come, good sir, will you show me to this house?
                                        Exeunt.

JESSICA: I would out-night you, did no body come;
30   But, hark, I hear the footing of a man.

Enter Messenger [Stephano].

LORENZO: Who comes so fast in silence of the night?
MESSENGER: A friend.
LORENZO: A friend? what friend? your name, I pray you,
            friend?
35 MESSENGER: Stephano is my name; and I bring word
            My mistress will before the break of day
            Be here at Belmont; she doth stray about
            By holy crosses, where she kneels and prays
            For happy wedlock hours.
40 LORENZO: Who comes with her?
    MESSENGER: None, but a holy hermit, and her maid.
            I pray you, is my master yet return'd?
    LORENZO: He is not, nor we have not heard from him.—
            But go we in, I pray thee, Jessica,
45   And ceremoniously let us prepare
            Some welcome for the mistress of the house.

[Enter Launcelot]

LAUNCELOT: Sola,† sola! wo ha, ho! sola, sola!
LORENZO: Who calls?
LAUNCELOT: Sola! did you see Master Lorenzo, and Mistress
50 Lorenzo? sola, sola!
    LORENZO: Leave hollaing, man; here.³
    LAUNCELOT: Sola! Where? where?
    LORENZO: Here.
    LAUNCELOT: Tell him there's a post come from my master,
55   with his horn full of good news; my master will be here
            ere morning.
    LORENZO: Sweet soul, let's in, and there expect their coming;
            And yet no matter:—why should we go in?
            My friend Stephano, signify, I pray you,
60   Within the house, your mistress is at hand:
            And bring your music forth into the air.
            How sweet the moonlight sleeps upon this bank!
            Here will we sit, and let the sounds of music
            Creep in our ears; soft stillness, and the night,

"Stop hollering, man. I'm here."

ACT V

[SCENE I]
[Belmont]

Enter Lorenzo and Jessica.

LORENZO: The moon shines bright:—in such a night as this,
When the sweet wind did gently kiss the trees,
And they did make no noise,—in such a night,
Troilus,† methinks, mounted the Trojan walls,
5   And sigh'd his soul toward the Grecian tents,
Where Cressid† lay that night.

JESSICA: In such a night,
Did Thisbe† fearfully o'ertrip the dew,
And saw the lion's shadow ere himself,
10   And ran dismay'd away.

LORENZO: In such a night,
Stood Dido,† with a willow in her hand,
Upon the wild sea-banks, and waft her love
To come again to Carthage.[1]

15 JESSICA: In such a night,
Medea† gather'd the enchanted herbs
That did renew old Æson.†

LORENZO: In such a night,
Did Jessica steal from the wealthy Jew,
20   And with an unthrift[2] love did run from Venice,
As far as Belmont.

JESSICA: In such a night,
Did young Lorenzo swear he lov'd her well;
Stealing her soul with many vows of faith,
25   And ne'er a true one.

LORENZO: In such a night,
Did pretty Jessica, like a little shrew,
Slander her love, and he forgave it her.

[1] *an imp...*
Phoeni...

[2] *wastefu...*
agant

65　Become the touches of sweet harmony.
　　Sit, Jessica. Look how the floor of heaven
　　Is thick inlaid with patines of bright gold.
　　There's not the smallest orb which thou behold'st,
　　But in his motion like an angel sings,
70　Still quiring[4] to the young-eyed cherubins:　　　　　　　[4]*choiring, singing*
　　Such harmony is in immortal souls;
　　But, whilst this muddy vesture of decay†
　　Doth grossly close it in, we cannot hear it.—
　　Come, ho! and wake Diana with a hymn;
75　With sweetest touches pierce your mistress' ear,
　　And draw her home with music.　　　　　　*Play music.*

JESSICA:　I am never merry when I hear sweet music.
LORENZO:　The reason is, your spirits are attentive:
　　For do but note a wild and wanton herd,
80　Or race of youthful and unhandled colts,
　　Fetching mad bounds, bellowing, and neighing loud,
　　Which is the hot condition of their blood,
　　If they but hear, perchance, a trumpet sound,
　　Or any air of music touch their ears,
85　You shall perceive them make a mutual stand,
　　Their savage eyes turn'd to a modest gaze,
　　By the sweet power of music. Therefore, the poet
　　Did feign that Orpheus† drew trees, stones and floods;†
　　Since nought so stockish,[5] hard, and full of rage,　　[5]*"nothing so solid"*
90　But music for the time doth change his nature.
　　The man that hath no music in himself,
　　Nor is not mov'd with concord of sweet sounds,　　　　[6]*strategies, plans*
　　Is fit for treasons, stratagems,[6] and spoils;[7]
　　The motions of his spirit are dull as night,　　　　　[7]*robbing, plundering*
95　And his affections dark as Erebus:†
　　Let no such man be trusted.—Mark the music.

Enter Portia and Nerissa.

PORTIA:　That light we see is burning in my hall:
　　How far that little candle throws his beams!
　　So shines a good deed in a naughty world.
100 NERISSA:　When the moon shone, we did not see the candle.
PORTIA:　So doth the greater glory dim the less:
　　A substitute shines brightly as a king,
　　Unto the king be by; and then his state,

Empties itself, as doth an inland brook
105   Into the main of waters. Music! hark!
NERISSA: It is your music, madam, of the house.
PORTIA: Nothing is good, I see, without respect;
        Methinks it sounds much sweeter than by day.
NERISSA: Silence bestows that virtue on it, madam.
110 PORTIA: The crow doth sing as sweetly as the lark,
        When neither is attended; and, I think,
        The nightingale, if she should sing by day,
        When every goose is cackling, would be thought
        No better a musician than the wren.
115   How many things by season season'd are
        To their right praise and true perfection![8]—
        Peace, ho! the moon sleeps with Endymion,[†]
        And would not be awak'd.   *Music ceases.*
LORENZO: That is the voice,
120   Or I am much deceiv'd, of Portia.
PORTIA: He knows me as the blind man knows the cuckoo,
        By the bad voice.
LORENZO: Dear lady, welcome home.
PORTIA: We have been praying for our husbands' welfare,
125   Which speed, we hope, the better for our words.
        Are they return'd?
LORENZO: Madam, they are not yet;
        But there is come a messenger before,
        To signify their coming.
130 PORTIA: Go in, Nerissa;
        Give order to my servants, that they take
        No note at all of our being absent hence;
        Nor you, Lorenzo:—Jessica, nor you.   *A tucket sounds.*
LORENZO: Your husband is at hand; I hear his trumpet:
135   We are no tell-tales,[9] madam; fear you not.
PORTIA: This night, methinks, is but the daylight sick.
        It looks a little paler; 'tis a day,
        Such as the day is, when the sun is hid.

Enter Bassanio, Antonio, Gratiano, and their followers.

BASSANIO: We should hold day with the Antipodes,[†]
140   If you would walk in absence of the sun.
PORTIA: Let me give light, but let me not be light;
        For a light wife doth make a heavy husband,

[8]*"In proper time, everything is praised and perfect."*

[9]*tattletales, snitches*

And never be Bassanio so for me:
But God sort all!—You are welcome home, my lord.
145 BASSANIO: I thank you, madam: Give welcome to my friend.—
This is the man, this is Antonio,
To whom I am so infinitely bound.
PORTIA: You should in all sense be much bound to him.
For, as I hear, he was much bound for you.
150 ANTONIO: No more than I am well acquitted of.
PORTIA: Sir, you are very welcome to our house:
It must appear in other ways than words,
Therefore, I scant this breathing courtesy.
GRATIANO: By yonder moon, I swear you do me wrong;
155 In faith, I gave it to the judge's clerk:
Would he were gelt[10] that had it, for my part,
Since you do take it, love, so much at heart.
PORTIA: A quarrel, ho, already! what's the matter?
GRATIANO: About a hoop of gold, a paltry ring
160 That she did give me; whose posy[11] was
For all the world, like cutler's poetry
Upon a knife, Love me, and leave me not!
NERISSA: What talk you of the posy, or the value?
You swore to me, when I did give it you,
165 That you would wear it till your hour of death;
And that it should lie with you in your grave:
Though not for me, yet for your vehement oaths,
You should have been respective, and have kept it.
Gave it a judge's clerk!—no, God's my judge!
170 The clerk will ne'er wear hair on's face that had it.
GRATIANO: He will, an if he live to be a man.
NERISSA: Ay, if a woman live to be a man.
GRATIANO: Now, by this hand, I gave it to a youth,—
A kind of boy; a little scrubbed boy,
175 No higher than thyself, the judge's clerk;
A prating boy, that begg'd it as a fee;
I could not for my heart deny it him.
PORTIA: You were to blame, I must be plain with you,
To part so slightly with your wife's first gift;
180 A thing stuck on with oaths upon your finger,
And so riveted with faith unto your flesh.
I gave my love a ring, and made him swear
Never to part with it; and here he stands,—
I dare be sworn for him he would not leave it,

[10]*castrated*

[11]*motto*

185   Nor pluck it from his finger, for the wealth
        That the world masters. Now, in faith, Gratiano,
        You give your wife too unkind a cause of grief;
        An 'twere to me, I should be mad at it.
BASSANIO: Why, I were best to cut my left hand off
190   And swear I lost the ring defending it.
GRATIANO: My Lord Bassanio gave his ring away
        Unto the judge that begg'd it, and, indeed,
        Deserv'd it too; and then the boy, his clerk,
        That took some pains in writing, he begg'd mine:
195   And neither man, nor master, would take aught
        But the two rings.
PORTIA: What ring gave you my lord?
        Not that, I hope, which you receiv'd of me.
BASSANIO: If I could add a lie unto a fault,
200   I would deny it; but you see, my finger
        Hath not the ring upon it, it is gone.
PORTIA: Even so void is your false heart of truth.
        By heaven, I will ne'er come in your bed
        Until I see the ring.
205 NERISSA: Nor I in yours
        Till I again see mine.
BASSANIO: Sweet Portia,
        If you did know to whom I gave the ring,
        If you did know for whom I gave the ring,
210   And would conceive for what I gave the ring,
        And how unwillingly I left the ring,
        When nought would be accepted but the ring,
        You would abate the strength of your displeasure.
PORTIA: If you had known the virtue of the ring,
215   Or half her worthiness that gave the ring,
        Or your own honour to contain the ring,
        You would not then have parted with the ring.
        What man is there so much unreasonable,
        If you had pleas'd to have defended it
220   With any terms of zeal, wanted the modesty
        To urge the thing held as a ceremony?
        Nerissa teaches me what to believe;
        I'll die for't, but some woman had the ring.
BASSANIO: No, by mine honour, madam, by my soul,
        No woman had it, but a civil doctor,
        Which did refuse three thousand ducats of me

And begg'd the ring; the which I did deny him,
And suffer'd him to go displeas'd away;
225   Even he that had uphold the very life
Of my dear friend. What should I say, sweet lady?
I was enforc'd to send it after him;
I was beset with shame and courtesy;
My honour would not let ingratitude
230   So much besmear it. Pardon me, good lady;
For, by these blessed candles of the night,
Had you been there, I think, you would have begg'd
The ring of me to give the worthy doctor.
PORTIA: Let not that doctor e'er come near my house:
235   Since he hath got the jewel that I lov'd,
And that which you did swear to keep for me,
I will become as liberal as you;
I'll not deny him any thing I have,
No, not my body, nor my husband's bed:
240   Know him I shall, I am well sure of it:
Lie not a night from home; watch me, like Argus;[†]
If you do not, if I be left alone,
Now, by mine honour, which is yet mine own,
I'll have that doctor for my bedfellow.
245 NERISSA: And I his clerk; therefore be well advis'd
How you do leave me to mine own protection.
GRATIANO: Well, do you so: let not me take him then,
For if I do, I'll mar[12] the young clerk's pen.
ANTONIO: I am the unhappy subject of these quarrels.
250 PORTIA: Sir, grieve not you; you are welcome notwithstanding.
BASSANIO: Portia, forgive me this enforced wrong;
And, in the hearing of these many friends,
I swear to thee, even by thine own fair eyes,
Wherein I see myself,—
255 PORTIA: Mark you but that!
In both my eyes he doubly sees himself:
In each eye, one:—swear by your double self,
And there's an oath of credit.
BASSANIO: Nay, but hear me:
260   Pardon this fault, and by my soul I swear,
I never more will break an oath with thee.
ANTONIO: I once did lend my body for his wealth;
Which, but for him that had your husband's ring,
Had quite miscarried: I dare be bound again,

[12]*ruin*

265   My soul upon the forfeit, that your lord
        Will never more break faith advisedly.

[13] *guarantee*

PORTIA: Then you shall be his surety.[13] Give him this
        And bid him keep it better than the other.

ANTONIO: Here, Lord Bassanio; swear to keep this ring.

270 BASSANIO: By heaven, it is the same I gave the doctor!

PORTIA: I had it of him: pardon me, Bassanio:
        For by this ring the doctor lay with me.

NERISSA: And pardon me, my gentle Gratiano;
        For that same scrubbed boy, the doctor's clerk,

275   In lieu of this last night did lie with me.

GRATIANO: Why, this is like the mending of highways
        In summer, where the ways are fair enough:
        What! are we cuckolds, ere we have deserv'd it?

PORTIA: Speak not so grossly.—You are all amaz'd:

280   Here is a letter; read it at your leisure;
        It comes from Padua, from Bellario:
        There you shall find that Portia was the doctor;
        Nerissa there, her clerk: Lorenzo here
        Shall witness, I set forth as soon as you,

285   And but e'en now return'd; I have not yet
        Enter'd my house.—Antonio, you are welcome;
        And I have better news in store for you,
        Than you expect: unseal this letter soon;
        There you shall find, three of your argosies

290   Are richly come to harbour suddenly:
        You shall not know by what strange accident
        I chanced on this letter.

[14] *speechless, dumbfounded*

ANTONIO: I am dumb.[14]

BASSANIO: Were you the doctor, and I knew you not?

295 GRATIANO: Were you the clerk that is to make me cuckold?

NERISSA: Ay, but the clerk that never means to do it,
        Unless he live until he be a man.

BASSANIO: Sweet doctor, you shall be my bedfellow;
        When I am absent, then lie with my wife.

300 ANTONIO: Sweet lady, you have given me life, and living;
        For here I read for certain, that my ships
        Are safely come to road.

PORTIA: How now, Lorenzo?
        My clerk hath some good comforts too for you.

305 NERISSA: Ay, and I'll give them him without a fee.—
        There do I give to you and Jessica,

From the rich Jew, a special deed of gift,
After his death, of all he dies possess'd of.
LORENZO: Fair ladies, you drop manna[15] in the way
310   Of starved people.
PORTIA: It is almost morning,
And yet, I am sure, you are not satisfied
Of these events at full. Let us go in;
And charge us there upon inter'gatories,
315   And we will answer all things faithfully.
GRATIANO: Let it be so. the first inter'gatory,
That my Nerissa shall be sworn on, is,
Whether till the next night she had rather stay,
Or go to bed now, being two hours to day:
320   But were the day come, I should wish it dark,
That I were couching with the doctor's clerk.
Well, while I live, I'll fear no other thing
So sore, as keeping safe Nerissa's ring.

                                          Exeunt.

[15]*miraculous food*†

Glossary

Act I, Scene I

Andrew – the name of Antonio's ship

"…her high-top…ribs…" – most likely, the ship is lying in the sand on its side with the tallest sail lower than the side

Janus – the Roman god of doors and entrances who had two faces each looking in opposite directions from the other, symbolizing beginnings and endings

Nestor – an advisor to the Greeks noted for his solemnity and gravity

"…neat's tongue…vendible." – "…a dried calf's tongue and a woman who can't get a husband."

"showing…grant continuance" – "spending more money than I can afford to, thereby appearing wealthier than I am"

Jasons – In Greek mythology, Jason searched for the valuable Golden Fleece.

Act I, Scene II

"That he hath a neighbourly…for another." – The Scottish lord received a box on the ears from the English suitor, and the French suitor promised to repay that blow to the Englishman.

Sibylla – Sibylla's were prophetesses; the Greek writer Heraclitus wrote of the Sibyl who could see a thousand years into the future with God's assistance.

Diana – In Roman mythology, Diana was the virgin goddess of childbirth as well as of hunting

"I had rather…wive me." – Portia would prefer to have the fifth man hear her confession and grant absolution, rather than marry him.

Act I, Scene III

Rialto – the business center of Venice

Nazarite – an individual of Jewish faith who vows to live a life of purity in an effort to show his or her devotion to God

Act II, Scene I

Phoebus' fire – In Greek mythology, Phoebus, also knows as Apollo, was god of the sun.

"Sophy" – "Sophy" is another name for the Emperor of Persia.

Sultan Solyman – a reference to Suleiman the Magnificent (1520 – 1566), sultan of the Ottoman Empire.

Hercules and Lichas – According to Greek mythology, Lichas was Hercules' servant and also the person responsible for poisoning and killing Hercules.

Alcides – another name for Hercules

Act II, Scene II

sisters three – the three Fates that affected a person's life: Atropos, Clothos, and Lachesis

affection or *desire* – Old Gobbo's malapropism is a direct stab at his own son's occupation. Instead of using "affection" or "desire" to describe Launcelot's passion for serving, Old Gobbo's use of "infection" puts an entirely different connotation on the statement. "Infection" suggests something unavoidable and malignant.

"a dish of doves" – Because doves are a sign of peace, offering someone a "dish of doves" illustrates an offering of a peaceful relationship or beginning

twinkling – neither the folio or quarto includes "of and eye."

Act II, Scene III

—

Act II, Scene IV

—

Act II, Scene V

Black-Monday – In 1360, on Easter Monday, the weather was so unusual that many men died from exposure to severe cold.

Jewess – a Jewish female

Hagar's offspring – a Christian and an outcast

"...drones hive not with me..." – Drones are male bees that typically do no work. Notice Shakespeare's play on "drones" and "hive."

Act II, Scene VI

Venus' pigeons – a reference to Roman mythology, in which Venus, goddess of vegetation, rides in a chariot drawn by doves

prodigal – a reference to the "prodigal son" in the Bible, who wasted his fortune

Cupid – Roman god of love

Act II, Scene VII

—

Act II, Scene VIII

—

Act II, Scene IX

—

Act III, Scene I

"carrion...years?" – The comment seems to show that Solanio is being insulting by
wondering if Shylock's flesh and bones are rebelling because of old age.

Act III, Scene II

"Beshrew your eyes…" – "Curse your eyes…" This use of "beshrew" is not a harsh
oath to Bassanio. It is a gentle admonishment.

"I live upon the rack." – The "rack" was used to torture criminals or traitors.

"a swan-like end" – It was believed that swans never made a sound until right before
their death.

"…when he did…To the sea-monster:" – rescued the virgin from the sea-monster

Mars – In Roman mythology, Mars is the god of war.

"livers white as milk" – The liver was considered to house an individual's courage;
whiteness indicates loss of blood and, therefore, cowardice. Bassanio then is saying that the men are all cowards.

valour's excrement – Beards were worn to give the appearance of strength and brav-
ery; the "excrement" seems to refer to hair being pushed out of the face to form
a beard.

"Hard food for Midas" – a reference to King Midas whose touch turned everything
to gold

"We are…won the fleece." – a reference to the story in Greek mythology in which
Jason and the Argonauts went on a quest to find the fleece to crown Jason king
of Iolcus.

Act III, Scene III

—

Act III, Scene IV

a reed voice – Reed suggests the thin piece of wood used in the mouthpiece of several
woodwind instruments (clarinets, oboes, saxophone, etc.). Shakespeare's pun on
the word reed suggests that Portia will disguise her voice with a kind of "piping"
voice.

turn to men – Nerissa's statement suggests a lewd interpretation, in that she thought
they would turn to men for sex

Act III, Scene V

"Scylla…Charybdis" – from Greek mythology, the two dangers, a sea monster named
Scylla, and a whirlpool, Charybdis, that ships must avoid to proceed safely on
their journey

pork-eaters – Jews were forbidden from eating pork.

Act IV, Scene I

Pythagoras – a Greek philosopher and mathematician from the sixth century B.C., who believed in the transmigration of souls.

Daniel – a reference to the Book of Daniel in the Bible. Daniel rescued Susanna from being falsely accused.

Act IV, Scene II

—

Act V, Scene I

Troilus; Cressid; Thisbe; Dido; Medea; Æson – These six characters from Greek mythology refer to famous love stories that have unhappy endings.

sola – a shout to attract attention; "Hello!"

"muddy vesture of decay" – a reference to the human body, comparing it to the human soul

Orpheus – a famous musician that is discussed in Ovid's well known *Metamorphoses*

"...therefore the poet...stones and floods;..." – "According to Ovid, Orpheus' music was so sweet it could make trees, stones, and floods pay attention."

Erebus – In Greek mythology, Erebus was a very dark area between life and death, Earth and Hades.

Endymion – In Greek mythology, the goddess of the moon, Selene, was madly in love with Endymion. Endymion was granted infinite youth by being inflicted with eternal slumber.

Antipodes – people living on the other side of the globe; during Shakespeare's time, many Elizabethans believe that a country existed on the opposite side of the earth where people were built upside down and walked with their feet in the air.

Argus – a creature from mythology that had one hundred eyes and was ordered to keep watch on the maiden, Io.

manna – a reference to the Bible story in which miraculous food appeared to the starving Israelites who were fleeing Egypt

Vocabulary

Act I, Scene I
ague – a fever and shaking caused by an illness; a fit
argosies – large merchant ships
gaged – pledged; bound to
gear – an affair, event
gudgeon – an easily caught fish
portly – filled; fat
presages – foretells
signiors – rich, powerful men; a term of respect

Act I, Scene II
appropriation – an assumption
ere – before
rhenish – a type of German wine
superfluity – excessiveness; having too much
surfeit – overindulgence
vilely – detestably, disgustingly, horridly

Act I, Scene III
eanlings – lambs, kids
fulsome – lustful
imputation – negative charges, incriminations
publican – a tax collector
squandered – scattered

Act II, Scene I
livery – a uniform, clothing
valiant – brave

Act II, Scene II
allay – to relieve
cater-cousins – not great friends
cudgel – a club
demurely – shyly
ergo – therefore
frutify – certify
sand-blind – dim-sighted
sonties – saints

Act II, Scene III - Act II, Scene IV
—

Act II, Scene V
fife – a type of flute
foppery – silliness
gormandise – to eat greedily
masque – a masquerade, costume party
prodigal – extremely wasteful

Act II, Scene VI
abode – a delay
scarfed – decorated with
untread – retrace

Act II, Scene VII
cerecloth – a cloth used in embalming
immured – imprisoned

Act II, Scene VIII
amorous – devoted
miscarried – failed; wrecked

Act II, Scene IX
alighted – dismounted
anon – immediately
chaff – straw
commends – compliments
courteous breath – flattery
injunctions – commands, directions
martlet – a type of bird
merit – excellence
new-varnish'd – glossed over
pries – investigates
solemnized – performed

Act III, Scene I
aloof – apart, away from
amity – friendships, relationships
deliverance – a rescue
entreat – to beg
fledged – left the nest

magnificoes – noblemen
monarch – a king, ruler
oration – a speech
plies – offers
ratified – approved
surfeit – overindulgence
trebled – tripled

Act III, Scene II
naughty – worthless, bad
prove – ascertain; find it so

Act III, Scene III
gaoler – a jail keeper
intercessors – mediators
relent – to weaken

Act III, Scene IV
accoutred – dressed
frays – fights, battles
lewd – dirty (sexual connotation)
lineaments – physical features
semblance – a representation; duplicate

Act III, Scene V
—

Act IV, Scene I
abject – wretched
acquitted – found innocent, not guilty
adversary – an enemy
attribute – a characteristic
carrion – dead
charter – a legal document
coffer – the treasury
commiseration – pity
contrive – to conspire
epitaph – the writing on a tombstone
exposition – an explanation
fretten – to agitate
gallows – a structure built and used for hanging criminals
impediment – an obstacle

inexecrable – unwavering; relentless
manifest – evident
mercenary – motivated by material gain, monetary
obdurate – inflexible
penance – misery
perjury – a false testimony (usually deliberate)
pillar – an individual with a highly responsible or authoritative occupation (the judge)
precedent – a decision made by a judge that may be used in similar cases
privy – a legal term in which one of the parties has an interest in the same case
recant – to withdraw
reverend – worthy of adoration
sceptre – a ruling authority
scruple – a reservation, qualm
temporal – earthly
tenor – the precise wording of a legal document
trifle – something of little value

Act IV, Scene II

—

Act V, Scene I
bounds – leaps
cherubins – angels
concord – harmonies, melodies
cutler – one who creates, repairs, and sells knives
feign – to imagine
inter'gatories – those questions asked in court that the defendant is obliged to answer
paltry – measly
patines – tiles
prating – talkative, chatty
riveted – fascinated
scant – to limit, stop
shrew – a type of mouse
slander – to defame; to make negative comments about a person's reputation
tucket – a trumpet
vehement – forceful, chatty
wanton – playful
wedlock – marriage
zeal – enthusiasm